International  English

Managing Change

Fiona Mee

DELTA Publishing
Quince Cottage
Hoe Lane
Peaslake
Surrey GU5 9SW
England

York Associates
Peasholme House
St Saviours Place
York YO1 7PJ
England

www.deltapublishing.co.uk

© DELTA Publishing and York Associates 2013

All rights reserved. No reproduction, copy or transmission of this publication may be made without written permission from the publishers or in accordance with the provisions of the Copyright, Designs and Patents Act 1988, or under the terms of any licence permitting copying issued by the Copyright Licensing Agency, Saffron House, 6–10 Kirby Street, London EC1N 8TS.

First published 2013

Edited by Catriona Watson-Brown
Designed by Caroline Johnston
Photos and cartoons by Cartoonstock (pages 19, 29, 40, 59, 79); Havaianas (page 53); iStock (pages 11, 22, 35, 45, 49, 50, 55 (top and bottom), 75, 78, 83, 85); Shutterstock (pages 8, 12, 15, 25, 30, 33, 38, 54, 55 (middle), 61, 62 Dongliu/Shutterstock.com, 64, 68, 70, 73, 80)
Cover photo © Getty
Cover design by Clare Webber
Printed in Greece by Bakis

ISBN 978-1-905085-68-2

Acknowledgements
The author would like to thank the following people for their help during the writing of the book: Jeremy Comfort, Steve Flinders, Bob Dignen, Jackie Black and Jon Dyson for all their help, and my family and the YA team for tolerating my lack of attention whilst I was absorbed in writing. Also Catriona Watson-Brown and Chris Hartley for all their support and patience.

The author and publishers are grateful to the following for permission to reproduce copyright material:
Guardian News and Media Ltd. for an adapted extract from the article *Wall Street crisis: Lehman staff and their stories* by David Teather, James Orr and Kathryn Hopkins, *The Guardian*, 16 September 2008, copyright Guardian News & Media Ltd. 2008; Steven McCabe for an adapted extract from his article *The Rise and Fall of Kodak – what went wrong?*, http://blogs.birminghampost.net/business/2012/01/the-rise-and-fall-of-kodak---w.html, 23 January 2012; Spiegel-Verlag for an adapted extract from *Changing the corporate culture: Microsoft reaps the rewards of female managers* by Michaela Schiessl, http://www.spiegel.de/international/business/changing-the-corporate-culture-microsoft-reaps-the-rewards-of-female-managers-a-533852.html, Spiegel Online International; York Associates for an adapted extract from 'Defining roles in an international team' in *The Mindful International Manager* by Jeremy Comfort and Peter Franklin, pub. York Associates.

In some instances we have been unable to trace the owners of copyright material and we would appreciate any information that would enable us to do so.

Contents

Introduction	4
Learning diary	5
Needs analysis	6

1 Change happens
- A Discussion and listening — 8
- B Communication skills: Clarifying information and listening actively — 10
- C Professional skills: Creating a sense of urgency — 12
- D Intercultural competence: Understanding differences in company culture — 14
  - Case study: Managing change at Friedmann Brothers — 15
- E Language reference — 16
- F Change-management tips and personal action plan — 17

2 Why change?
- A Discussion and listening — 18
- B Communication skills: Discussing change strategy — 20
- C Professional skills: Making the case for change — 22
- D Intercultural competence: Communicating a vision across cultures — 24
  - Case study: Adapting a change strategy in China — 25
- E Language reference — 26
- F Change-management tips and personal action plan — 27

3 Communicating change
- A Discussion and listening — 28
- B Communication skills: Using the right language — 30
- C Professional skills: Communicating clearly in a crisis — 32
- D Intercultural competence: Developing flexibility in communication style — 34
  - Case study: Communicating change across borders — 35
- E Language reference — 36
- F Change-management tips and personal action plan — 37

4 Overcoming resistance
- A Discussion and listening — 38
- B Communication skills: Dealing with resistance — 40
- C Professional skills: Dealing with the consequences of redundancies — 42
- D Intercultural competence: Understanding motivation across cultures — 44
  - Case study: Overcoming resistance — 45
- E Language reference — 46
- F Change-management tips and personal action plan — 47

5 Influencing people
- A Discussion and listening — 48
- B Communication skills: Using influencing skills — 50
- C Professional skills: Influencing people through storytelling — 52
- D Intercultural competence: Influencing people across cultures — 54
  - Case study: Influencing a new team in Brazil — 55
- E Language reference — 56
- F Change-management tips and personal action plan — 57

6 Developing change leaders
- A Discussion and listening — 58
- B Communication skills: Giving and receiving feedback — 60
- C Professional skills: Training for change — 62
- D Intercultural competence: Developing change leaders across cultures — 64
  - Case study: Developing people through feedback internationally — 65
- E Language reference — 66
- F Change-management tips and personal action plan — 67

7 Evaluating and measuring
- A Discussion and listening — 68
- B Communication skills: Asking SMART questions — 70
- C Professional skills: Monitoring change through social media — 72
- D Intercultural competence: Measuring success across cultures — 74
  - Case study: Changing project management — 75
- E Language reference — 76
- F Change-management tips and personal action plan — 77

8 Cultural shifts
- A Discussion and listening — 78
- B Communication skills: Presenting arguments — 80
- C Professional skills: Changing business culture — 82
- D Intercultural competence: Building diverse teams — 84
  - Case study: Candidate selection — 85
- E Language reference — 86
- F Change-management tips and personal action plan — 87

Activity file	88
Audio script	96
Answer key	107
Word list	118

Introduction

At York Associates, we always aim to develop the skills which help professionals to do their jobs better. In recent years, we have worked hard to enrich our Business English and professional communication training with intercultural content. More recently, we have included a focus on important interpersonal and management skills for listening, building relationships and trust, influencing, etc.

Our approach is built on the premise that good communication is vital to achieving results at work. Effective international communicators need a blend of language, professional communication, intercultural and management skills to be successful.

Welcome to *International Management English*, a new series published jointly by York Associates and Delta Publishing. The four titles in this series are:
- *Leading People*
- *Managing Projects*
- *Working Virtually*
- *Managing Change*

Each book includes either one or two audio CDs.

Professional language training with a management focus

Each book consists of eight units of study, containing four sections per unit:
- *Section A: Discussion and listening*
  Engaging and relevant content in areas of international management and teamwork
- *Section B: Communication skills*
  Opportunities for the practice of key skills in areas such as conflict management, team-building and giving/receiving feedback, as well as more familiar topics such as presentations, meetings, negotiations and writing e-mails
- *Section C: Professional skills*
  Authentic texts from leading management writers and thinkers, designed to encourage reflection and debate among readers
- *Section D: Intercultural competence and Case study*
  A focus on raising intercultural awareness, followed by an illustrative case study drawn from the author's experience of the international business world

In addition, each unit offers:
- a strong emphasis on vocabulary learning, with glossaries of key terms at the end of each unit
- practical tips on how to improve performance at work
- the opportunity to use a learning diary, which encourages the setting of realistic goals to implement the learning points from each unit

At the end of the book, the Word list provides a useful list of key words, referenced to the first occurrence of each word.

Having worked through the book, you will have developed not only your business language skills but also your ability to communicate and manage real challenges in your international working environment.

To the teacher

The four titles in this series represent a new development in ELT. They broaden the scope of teaching to include highly relevant management topics and skills. The materials are not only engaging for teachers, allowing them to introduce and develop new management communication skills in an ELT classroom; students are also motivated as they learn how to manage real professional communication challenges which they face at work on a daily basis.

Each title is designed primarily for work with both small and larger groups, but can also be used in one-to-one situations and has many features which will support self-study.

Across the eight units of each title, there is a strong focus on developing fluency and skills to communicate effectively in real work situations. There are opportunities to practise listening, reading and writing skills. The intercultural case studies in Section D are drawn from real-life examples and provide engaging discussion and problem-solving material for the ELT classroom.

There is online support for trainers (www.delta publishing.co.uk/resources) in the form of notes for each unit, which provide background information on the management topics and skills presented.

A final word

To both learner and teacher, we would like to express the hope that you find the materials stimulating, and that they help people to communicate more effectively at work.

Learning diary

Accelerate your learning by using this Learning diary. Make eight photocopies of this page, one for each unit. Note down important new words and expressions from the unit as you study. Make notes to help you remember any good advice you get on how to communicate and be effective across cultures. Then decide on some actions you can take to help to consolidate the things you have learned.

Unit number: _____

1 Language
Important (new) words and expressions for me from this unit are:

2 Professional communication skills
Important (new) expressions and communication tips for me from this unit are:

3 Intercultural competence
Important information/tips to be effective across cultures for me from this unit are:

4 Actions
To help me to consolidate all the learning points above, I need to:

Needs analysis

Introduction You can use this Needs analysis to help you think about how to make the most of this course and to maximise your learning.

Managing your communication network Think about who you communicate with in English. Draw a diagram to represent your network of communications, showing the important individuals or groups of people you communicate with. Follow the example and then note down the channel of communication you use, e.g. face-to-face, phone, video conference, e-mail, etc.

How effectively do you use your network? Are you connecting with the right people in the best way at the most appropriate time? Are you spending enough time communicating with each individual or group?
Brainstorm some ideas for ways in which you could use your network more effectively.

I should spend more time planning my longer e-mails rather than writing them quickly and sending without considering the message. That way, I would get a more positive response from some colleagues.

Your communication needs What do you have to do in English, and how challenging is it? Build your own communication profile by completing the following tables for change-management skills, professional communication skills and interpersonal skills. Tick (✓) the tasks you most commonly do. Then note down how challenging you find them, using a scale of 1 to 5 (1 = very easy, 2 = easy, 3 = occasional problems, 4 = challenging, 5 = very difficult). If you score 3 or more for a task, write down a reason why it is challenging.

Change-management skills

skill	✓	scale of challenge
Creating a sense of urgency		
Developing a change strategy		
Communicating change		
Dealing with resistance		
Convincing others to accept change		
Developing change leaders		
Measuring and monitoring change		
Consolidating change		
Other		

Professional communication skills

skill	✓	scale of challenge
Presenting		
Meeting		
Negotiating		
Writing (reports, e-mails, etc.)		
Socialising		
Decision-making		
Problem-solving		
Other		

Interpersonal skills

skill	✓	scale of challenge
Building and maintaining relationships		
Networking		
Building and maintaining trust		
Influencing people		
Listening actively		
Managing conflict		
Other		

Your language and communication challenges

You manage change in an international context and you use a foreign language to do so. What are the biggest language and communication challenges that you face?

1 ....
2 ....
3 ....

Your intercultural challenges

What are the biggest intercultural challenges that you face?

1 ....
2 ....
3 ....

Your current learning objectives

What would most help you to improve your ability to communicate effectively in an international change-management context?

1 ....
2 ....
3 ....

Your future learning targets

As part of your learning plan, what targets can you fix for yourself? Start a learning diary (see page 5) and set yourself targets for future learning using this frame:

In one month's time, I aim to be able to ....
In three months' time, I aim to be able to ....
In six months' time, I aim to be able to ....
In one year's time, I aim to be able to ....

Needs analysis

Change happens

AIMS
A To identify contexts for change
B To clarify information and listen actively
C To create a sense of urgency
D To understand differences in company culture

A Discussion and listening

Think about it

> *The winners of tomorrow will deal proactively with chaos, will look at the chaos per se, as the source of market advantage, not as a problem.*
> Tom Peters (1942–), American business writer

1 **Discuss these questions with a partner.**
   a What kind of organisation do you work in? How big is it? What changes have you seen in it since you started working there?
   b What is your role in the organisation? How has your role changed since you joined the organisation?

2 **With a partner, complete the phrase below with three or four of your own ideas. Then compare with other pairs.**
   Change happens when an organisation … *becomes too large and complex.*

3 In his book *Thriving on Chaos*, Tom Peters says: 'If it ain't broke, you just haven't looked hard enough. Fix it anyway.' What does he mean? Do you agree with him?

Listen to this

4 🎧 **1** **Listen to an interview with Gilberto Ferreira, the CEO of a bank in Brazil, about a change at the bank, the impact it had on people, and how he managed it. Then answer these questions.**
   a What were three of the weaknesses Gilberto identified in his organisation?
   b What was his main reason for implementing change?
   c Why did some managers feel there was no need for change?
   d Why were the changes difficult for some mid-level executives?
   e What two pieces of advice does he give?

5 Do you have any experience of the kind of change described by Gilberto Ferreira? Would you add anything to the advice he gives? Discuss with a partner and write down your ideas.

Focus on language

> Look at this statement from the interview:
> *Innovation and the flow of ideas within the company were not as good. I thought that we needed to change this if we were going to maintain our competitive edge.*
> Change often happens when companies feel the need to increase their **innovation** and **performance** in order to remain **competitive**.

6 Complete each of these sentences with the correct form of the word *compete*.

   a Due to strong .... in mature markets, many companies are changing their strategy by moving into emerging BRIC countries (Brazil, Russia, India and China).
   b We keep ahead of our larger .... because we are a more flexible, innovative company with low overheads. This means we can respond to change more easily.
   c Managers increasingly need to .... in a global marketplace for the best positions. One essential competence is the ability to manage change.
   d In times of recession, ... organisations are likely to fail. This is often a sign that they have not adapted to change.

7 a Complete these collocations (a–f) with the correct form of the word *innovation*.

   a an .... manager
   b ....-driven growth
   c product ....
   d .... to survive
   e .... strategy
   f a leading ....

b Match each collocation above (a–f) with the correct definition (1–6).

   1 Implementing a strategy for increasing performance, often when it is considered that cost reductions and restructuring are not enough
   2 A specific plan to achieve innovation with milestones and targets in order to achieve commercial results
   3 A professional who successfully produces new ideas and ways of doing things, turning these into reality
   4 Making new things that are different to what is currently available
   5 A person or company that is ahead of others in creating new products and/or ways of doing things
   6 The belief that a company must continuously be looking for new and better ways to work in order to stay in business

Let's talk

8 Use these questions to interview your partner and make notes of their responses. When you are giving your answers, try to use as many of the terms from Exercises 6 and 7 as you can.

   a In your organisation, does your team engage in open debate? What can the advantages of this approach be in a change context?
   b How is innovation encouraged in your organisation/department/team?
   c Do you think you are an innovative manager? Give some examples.
   d What changes have you made in your department/organisation in order to maintain a competitive edge?
   e Have you ever had to make tough people decisions? Why did you / your organisation have to make this decision? How did you communicate it?
   f Have you ever struggled to adapt to a change? Why?

B Communication skills: Clarifying information and listening actively

Think about it

As business becomes more global, changes in the way people communicate are inevitable. Here are two examples of typical problems:
- Native speakers use complex or colloquial expressions that are not easily understood by non-native speakers.
- Non-native speakers who are not confident using English may pronounce words incorrectly.

Tip
Working in geographically dispersed teams can be challenging. As a first step, it can be useful to agree some communication guidelines.

1 a Can you think of any other communication problems caused by changes in how we communicate, the channels we use, or who we communicate with?

   b Compare your answers with the rest of the class and write your list on a board. Discuss any experience you have had of the problems on the list.

2 Work in groups. Brainstorm some solutions to one or two communication problems from the list in Exercise 1. Each group should brainstorm a different problem. Present your solutions to the other groups.

Listen to this

3 🎧 **2** Serge Manet is a French project manager for an international food company. A larger organisation has recently bought his and other smaller companies around the world as part of a global expansion strategy. Listen to him talking about the change this has caused in his part of the organisation and answer these questions.
   a What was the key change implemented?
   b What was the goal?

4 a 🎧 **3–5** Listen to comments from three members of Serge's team: Kristina (responsible for planning, based in Ingolstadt, Germany), Juana (project team member, based in Puebla, Mexico) and Tom (sales manager, based in Michigan, USA).

   b When Serge asked project members what impact they had experienced due to the changed ways of working, what three pieces of feedback did he get?

   c If you were Serge, what would you do as a result of this feedback? Discuss some ideas as a group and suggest some possible actions that he could take.

Focus on language

5 Complete each of the sentences below with a phrase for clarification from the box.

Tip
It's a good idea to use clarifying phrases in order to confirm understanding.

| When you say …   Could we clarify …   If I understand … |
| Just to confirm, what you're saying …   So are you saying … |

   a .... that if we work more as a global team, we'll achieve higher growth?
   b .... roles again? I thought that you were responsible for producing the project budget.
   c .... is we should have a web meeting every Monday at 9 a.m. to update the rest of the team on progress. Is that OK for everyone?
   d .... 'silos', do you mean different groups not really working well together, focusing on their own priorities?
   e .... you correctly, you didn't answer my e-mail because you prefer dealing with these questions by phone. Is that right?

6 Complete each of the sentences below with a phrase for establishing mutual understanding from the box.

> Can we establish the purpose   Firstly, I think we should agree
> We need to set down some rules   It must be clear who is responsible
> We should explain the reason

a .... on how often we need to communicate – it should be regular, but we need time between meetings to prepare.

b .... of each call in advance? I think it's important to have structured meetings, but also the occasional social call.

c .... about e-mail. I don't think we should use e-mail for any sensitive issues or negative feedback, for example.

d .... for not sharing information or answering questions – in cases, for example, where information is confidential or uncertain.

e .... for organising and monitoring the communication process.

Let's talk **7** Work in groups of four. You have just started working in the same cross-functional team whose purpose is to share innovative ideas and solutions to problems. You each have to collect ideas from your markets and bring them to a weekly meeting, where the team will choose the strongest ideas to present to top management in order to build new projects.

Student A: See below.
Student B: Turn to page 90.
Student C: Turn to page 94.
Student D: Turn to page 95.

Agree and draw up a list of communication guidelines for your team, then present them to the rest of the group. Try to use some of the language from Exercises 5 and 6 during your discussions.

> **Student A**
> **Catarina: Financial Controller**
> - You are based at the company's headquarters in Taipei.
> - You are already part of another key cross-functional team looking at cost savings, productivity and efficiency.
> - Due to the difficult financial climate, you are concerned about the short-term results of the company. You don't think now is the best time to focus on this kind of collaboration.
> - You don't think you'll have time for brainstorming or discussions, but think you can input financial data, as long as you are given a request in writing with detailed information and asked well in advance.

1 Change happens

C Professional skills: Creating a sense of urgency

Think about it 1 When a company is in serious financial difficulty, change managers need to be able to create a sense of urgency and to communicate how to deliver results. What personal experience, if any, do you have of this?

Read this 2 Read this extract from an interview with Michael Vianden, an interim manager who is brought in when companies are facing serious financial difficulties, and answer the questions on page 13.

Five years ago, I was brought in to a national airline which was spiralling out of control. The first thing I did was look at several years of financial data. In the end, everything comes down to the P&L. If you see that there are continuous patterns of losses and the company is not generating enough surplus cash, then there is trouble. Some people want to say that a company needs to change its culture or restructure because it's too big or too complex, but in the end, it's down to the P&L. You can't blame it on something vague like organisational design or culture and you don't have time to go through years of organisational changes.

In this particular organisation, I identified three big problems: low margins, inefficient networks and high costs. The cost of the service to customers was too low, some routes were being serviced on a regular basis at no more than 20% capacity, which made no commercial sense. The company had a large number of employees, but productivity was low, and costs had been increasing by 20% every year whilst the losses were also increasing.

Clearly, there were problems, but identifying the problems wasn't difficult; the issue was what do you do about it? We forecast that if we didn't turn things around in three months, the company would be bankrupt. So I just called the management to a meeting and said, 'We have no time to reorganise. If costs are too high, we have to cut them; if routes are inefficient, we have to stop running them; and if revenue is too low, we have to increase our prices.' I just said this is what we must do and we must do it now, not tomorrow or the day after. So we looked at all the products and services that were central to the business and we divided them into projects. I put a team of key people in each project group and made them accountable for solving the problem. If people understand the urgency of a situation and they're made responsible for the solution, you get fast results.

The next step was to make sure that people prioritised these actions. In times of crisis, it's not possible for people to say, 'Oh, but I'd really like to be focusing on something else' – you have to link everything to getting the desired results. So we linked pay increases and bonuses to each individual's contribution to the financial success of the organisation. Each employee had the responsibility to really focus their activities on the P&L, no more complacency or passivity.

As a consequence of this turnaround, the culture did change, people became more results driven, and now they take more responsibility, which is key to maintaining success.

a What three main problems did Michael Vianden identify when he joined the business?
b How did he implement change?
c How did he motivate people?
d How did he get across a sense of urgency regarding the need for change? Give some examples from the text that demonstrate this.
e At the end, he says that the culture changed. What exactly were people doing differently?
f Do you think Vianden had the right approach to people? Would you be motivated by his approach?

3 Match the words on the left (1–6) with those on the right (a–f) to make word pairs from the first two paragraphs of the article.

1 commercial   a costs
2 financial   b changes
3 high   c data
4 inefficient   d networks
5 low   e margins
6 organisational   f sense

Focus on language

You can use sentences with *if* + the present tense to talk about problems and solutions. Look at these examples from the text:
If routes are inefficient, we **have** *to stop running them.*
If revenue is too low, we **have** *to increase our prices.*

4 Complete each of the sentences below with a suitable verb from the box.

| change | link | make | prioritise | speak up |

a If you want people to deliver results, ... pay increases and bonuses to performance.
b If you don't agree with something, ... about it.
c If you don't want people to be complacent, ... the culture.
d If you want people to fix a problem, ... them accountable for it.
e If a task has an impact on the P&L, ... it.

5 Use these prompts in the correct order to write sentences using *If ... don't/doesn't ... will*.
a reduce / we / not / cut / costs / profits
b fail / not / change / the / company / urgently / it
c our country / implement / international trade agreements / business / lose / it
d sales / look for / new markets / not / our / organisation / drop

Let's talk

6 DGO is a global drinks company headquartered in London. Although the company has a turnover of more than $5 billion and profits of over $1.5 billion, the company has decided to close a plant in the UK, which supplies western and southern European markets. Senior management have already dealt with voluntary redundancies, and now the reduced local management team (who have agreed to relocate post-closure) must communicate this news to workers' representatives in the plant that will close.

Student A: Turn to page 88.
Student B: Turn to page 91.

D Intercultural competence: Understanding differences in company culture

1 Think of a company you know well. What three words would you use to describe its culture (e.g. *formal, hi-tech, traditional, entrepreneurial*)?

2 Match each of the phrases in the box describing a company culture with the description below (a–i) that best explains what it means.

> blame culture   ~~centralised decision-making~~   closed offices
> formal dress   hierarchical organisation   high-pressure atmosphere
> high-quality brand   results-oriented   strong values

a All our marketing plans are agreed at Head Office. *centralised decision-making*
b We all dress smartly and wear business suits.
c At the end of the quarter, the most important thing is the bottom line. We must reach our financial goals.
d People are competitive in our company. If we don't achieve, we risk losing our jobs.
e Our products are at the top end of the market.
f We don't have an 'open-door' policy. Managers are separate from other employees.
g This is an old company with a very clear idea of what is important for success.
h We have a command-and-control model of management.
i Mistakes are viewed very negatively. Those responsible have to pay.

Focus on language

3 Complete the paragraph below about culture and change using the correct form of the verbs from the box.

> act   behave   celebrate   change   enlist
> form   grow   not change   not work   value

Culture usually comes from the founders of a group. They (a) .... certain things and (b) .... in ways that help the group succeed. Culture (c) .... when a powerful person at the top or a large-enough group from the organisation decides the old ways (d) .... They start (e) .... differently and (f) .... others to act differently. If the new actions produce better results, if the results are communicated and (g) .... , if they are not stopped by the old culture fighting back, then new norms will (h) .... and new shared values will (i) .... Culture (j) .... when some group decides what the new culture should be and gives a list of values to the HR department with the order that they tell people what the new culture is.

4 Interview your partner about their working culture using these questions.
a How much freedom do employees have? Are they controlled and directed or encouraged to use their initiative and try new ideas?
b Is decision-making centralised or decentralised? Are decisions made quickly or slowly?
c Are there formal working hours, or is time more flexible? Is work based on completing tasks or numbers of hours?
d Do people dress formally or informally? Are offices open plan? Where do senior managers sit?
e Is there a strong feedback and development culture? Is there more focus on people or results?
f Has your company tried to change the culture since you've worked there, or have you noticed cultural changes taking place?
g What changes would you like to see in the company culture where you work (e.g. what things could be done in a different way, what changes might produce better results, what changes would improve employee motivation)?

Case study: Managing change at Friedmann Brothers

Background Friedmann Brothers was originally a traditional family business. Founded in 1895 in Germany, it produced supplies for postal services. Today, the headquarters are in Cincinnati, USA, and the company produces electronic parts for the telecoms industry. Tobias Friedmann is the head of the family and now acts as non-executive president. His grandson Joachim has recently taken over as CEO, following a period living and studying in Europe. Telecoms has enjoyed high growth in the last 20 years, and Joachim sees many new opportunities. As a result, the company has decided to invest in a programme of rapid globalisation through establishing sales subsidiaries and production plants in other countries. They now have significant units in Brazil, Poland and China.

Situation As part of general efficiency improvements, Joachim Friedmann has decided to streamline decision-making and communication across the organisation. He has asked his heads of department to review company structures and communication methods. In surveys, it has been established that the US organisation is quite hierarchical, decision-making is slow, communication is not efficient, and information is often difficult to obtain. Another measure being considered is to move more production from the US to China.

The Head of R&D in Cincinnati, Peter Ledblom, is quite resistant to changes in the structure of the company. He thinks some of the core values of the company, for example providing the highest-quality products, are being lost. He doesn't trust the team members in the other countries and is afraid to share too much information. He's also heard rumours about production moving to China, which worries him. He has a lot of influence in his department and across the company.

Tasks 1 **Work with a partner.**
Student A: See below.
Student B: Turn to page 91.

> **Student A**
> You are Stefano Visconti. You have been asked by Joachim Friedmann to have a meeting with Peter Ledblom. You have to convince Peter of the need to change and agree how this change should take place. Negotiate with Peter to agree an action plan. You don't want to talk about the move of production from the US to China at this stage. You may need to clearly express an urgent need to change the way things are done currently and that other changes may be necessary in order to ensure the future survival of the company.
> **Expected outcomes**
> - Agree a minimum timeframe from order to delivery which also ensures quality is maintained, ideally five weeks.
> - Gain agreement on necessity and time to answer questions / provide information.
> - Agree a schedule of regular meetings.

2 **After the role-play, meet as a group. Discuss and summarise the key changes that need to take place at Friedmann Brothers.**

E Language reference

Read through the key words and phrases below. Add any other useful words and expressions which you feel are important for you to learn. Make sure you find the time to review these words and phrases regularly and to use them at work.

Contexts for change

innovation	merger/acquisition
competition	inefficiency
financial crisis	low margins

Clarifying

So are you saying that ...?	When you say ... , do you mean ...?
Could you clarify ...?	If I understand you correctly, ...
Just to confirm, what you're saying is ...	

Establishing mutual understanding

Can we establish the purpose of ...?	It must be clear who is responsible for ...
Firstly, I think we should agree on ...	We should explain the reason for ...
We need to set down some rules about ...	

Summarising and checking

To sum up, ...	I think you are saying ...
If I can summarise the main points, ...	Would you agree that the key ideas are ...?
What I understand is ...	

Offering solutions

deliver results	prioritise
link pay increases to performance	cut costs
speak up about something	implement
fix a problem	look for new markets
make people accountable	

Differences in company cultures

hierarchical/flat **organisation**
centralised/decentralised/collaborative **decision-making**
results-/people-/innovation-**oriented**
formal/casual **dress**
closed-/open-plan **offices**
innovative/conservative/forward **thinking**
blame/development/technical/scientific **culture**
high-pressure/relaxed/professional/creative **atmosphere**
strong/traditional/modern **values**
high-quality/well-known/innovative/low-cost **brand**
bureaucratic/web/matrix/cluster **structure**

Writing task Choose one of these e-mail writing activities and try to use some of the language from above.

1 Your boss has asked if you could come into the office at eight instead of nine in future. The objective would be that the European units would have a fixed time to ask questions and get information before heading out each day to sales appointments, etc. You know that this will be impossible for you, as you need to take your children to school before coming to work. However, you could be available to answer e-mails and take phone calls from home from 6.30–7.30 p.m. (which would be 7.30–8.30 p.m. in Europe). Write an e-mail to your boss to try to establish mutual agreement on this. Take a constructive approach.

2 A new colleague is coming to join your team from another country. It's your responsibility to help this person integrate into the team and into the company. Write an e-mail to your new colleague. Introduce yourself and tell them about the way your company works, dress code, something about the way people communicate, important 'dos and don'ts'. Then tell them some specific information about the habits and ways things are done in your department and team. Be positive and welcoming.

F Change-management tips and personal action plan

1 **Take a few minutes to reflect on these tips on managing change which arise from this unit. How far do you agree with each one? Which do you think is the most important, and which ideas are the most useful?**

> **TIP 1**
> Change can mean many different things, from completely restructuring a company in response to a crisis, merger or acquisition to more gradual but continuous improvement programmes. Change can come from within the organisation or it can be pushed on it by external forces. Whatever the context, it's important not to be complacent – change is happening all the time.
> Ideas for coping with change:
> - Always look for new ideas and changes to your strategy, products or ways of doing things. Have a continuous log which everyone in your department or unit contributes to, and make sure you also get input from those in other locations.
> - Prioritise all the items in the log and use them for reference when goal setting and when putting forward proposals to management.

> **TIP 2**
> For many, work today involves regular changes in who we work with, where those people are located, and how we communicate with each other. In order to improve your efficiency, especially when under pressure, you need to maximise the effectiveness of your communication in order to achieve the best result in the shortest possible time.
> Ideas for improving communication:
> - Invest time initially to agree guidelines for communication.
> - Always clarify and check information to avoid misunderstandings and to make sure you haven't missed any details.
> - Summarise at the end of a communication, especially agreed actions and deadlines.

> **TIP 3**
> Companies can fail because the need for change is not communicated strongly enough or people don't believe change is necessary. As a change leader or change consultant, it is vital that you develop the right language to communicate urgency and find effective ways to convince people of the need for change.
> Ideas for communicating urgency:
> - Communicate the consequences of not changing in short, clear messages.
> - Give examples of worst-case scenarios and follow this up by offering solutions and clearly stating what needs to be done in order to be successful.

Personal action plan 2 **Take 15 minutes to review the unit. Write down at least three important points that you have learned and that you want to apply to your change-management practice. Then commit to a schedule to implement your learning and think about how you can check if you have been successful.**

	what I have learned and want to apply in my change-management practice	when/how I will apply this in my change-management practice	how I will check if I have applied it
1			
2			
3			

1 Change happens

2 Why change?

AIMS
A To identify threats and opportunities as causes for change
B To discuss change strategy
C To make the case for change
D To communicate a vision across cultures

A Discussion and listening

Think about it

> *If the rate of change on the outside exceeds the rate of change on the inside, the end is near.*
> Jack Welch (1935–), former chairman and CEO of General Electric

1 **Discuss these questions with a partner.**
  a What external change has had the greatest impact on your organisation in the last five years?
  b What external threats and opportunities do you think your organisation may face in the next five years?
  c How can organisations ensure that they adapt successfully to changes in the external environment?

Listen to this 2 🎧 **6** Laura Ortiz is the Global Marketing Manager for Radar, an international sports footwear retailer based in Zaragoza, Spain. Listen to her and one of her team, Stefan, presenting to a group of managers from a partner company how Radar reacted to a major external threat. Then answer these questions.
  a What external threat did the company's senior executives identify?
  b How did the company reduce costs?
  c What was the second issue the company faced?
  d Following the introduction of the new vision, what was the impact on sales?
  e In which three areas did the company invest?
  f What was the greatest barrier to getting the new strategy accepted?

3 **Complete the sentences below from Stefan and Laura's new marketing strategy using the phrases in the box.**

| in order to achieve | it's essential that we | our aim is | we will do this |

  a .... for every customer to have the ability to create and buy their dream shoe online, with good quality and at a price that suits their pocket.
  b .... this goal, we need empowered people and new technology. .... by thinking long term, investing in equipment and developing people's skills.
  c Going forward, ... develop a highly efficient, flexible organisation with adaptable people, who can change the way they do things to match the changing world.

Focus on language **4 a** Decide whether each of these concepts from Track 6 is a threat or an opportunity and write them in the appropriate column of the table below.

> ~~growing Asian competition~~   online purchasing   new technology
> low sales   ineffective marketing   computer-aided manufacturing (CAM)
> exposure to debt   developing new skills   high prices

threats	opportunities
growing Asian competition	

b Can you add any more of your own?

5 The verbs in the box can all be used with *threat* and/or *opportunity*. Complete the gaps in each of the sentences below with the appropriate form of one of the verbs.

> avoid   exploit   face   find out   identify
> ignore   miss   take   scan

a We .... a threat from foreign competition which we cannot ....
b We should .... this opportunity now, otherwise, we could .... it all together.
c Following some in-country research, we have .... an opportunity to expand into a new emerging market. I think we should seriously consider this option.
d The company has established a taskforce which constantly .... the internal and external environment for threats and opportunities.
e Networking, attending conferences and talking to people in different parts of the world are great ways to .... about new opportunities.
f Sometimes it's impossible to .... a threat to your business, so you have to have contingency plans in place to deal with the consequences.
g In order to .... this opportunity, we're going to need to take on more staff, otherwise we won't have the capacity.

Let's talk **6** Work with a partner.
- Share some of the main threats and opportunities facing your organisation today which you identified in Exercise 1. Ask your partner these questions to help you.
  – What good opportunities can you identify, for example related to changes in technology and markets, changes in government policy, lifestyle changes, etc.?
  – What interesting trends are you aware of?
  – What obstacles do you face? What are your competitors doing? Is changing technology threatening your position?
- Discuss ideas for both meeting the threats and exploiting the opportunities.
- Develop a plan for the changes needed in the organisation's culture to survive.
- Use some of the phrases from Exercise 3 to present your plan to the group, for example:
  Our aim is …
  In order to achieve this goal, we need to …
  Going forward, it's essential that we …

Henry couldn't help but have doubts about the future of the company.

2 Why change?

B Communication skills: Discussing change strategy

Think about it

1 Scenario planning is the process of imagining what future conditions or events are probable, deciding what their effects might be, and planning how best to respond to them. How do you think scenario planning can be useful for developing a change strategy?

2 Can you give an example of scenario planning from your professional or personal experience?

Listen to this

3 🎧 7 Agora is a successful small civil-engineering firm. It's in the process of passing on from the founding partners, who have retired, to the next stage of its development. Listen to Jon, Laurent and Liliana, the three remaining partners. They are debating a possible future scenario during a strategy meeting.
   a What problem does the company face, and why?
   b What is the scenario the partners are considering?
   c Can you identify two risks and two opportunities in the scenario being discussed?
   d What would you do if you were one of the partners?

4 Scenario planning involves three key skills. Complete the diagram below with these definitions of those skills (a–c).
   a Evaluation of the possible or probable effects of external forces and conditions on an organisation's survival and growth strategies
   b An expression of how an organisation needs to evolve over time to meet its objectives, along with a detailed assessment of what needs to be done
   c A planning tool that helps management in its attempts to cope with the uncertainty of the future, relying mainly on data from the past and present and analysis of trends

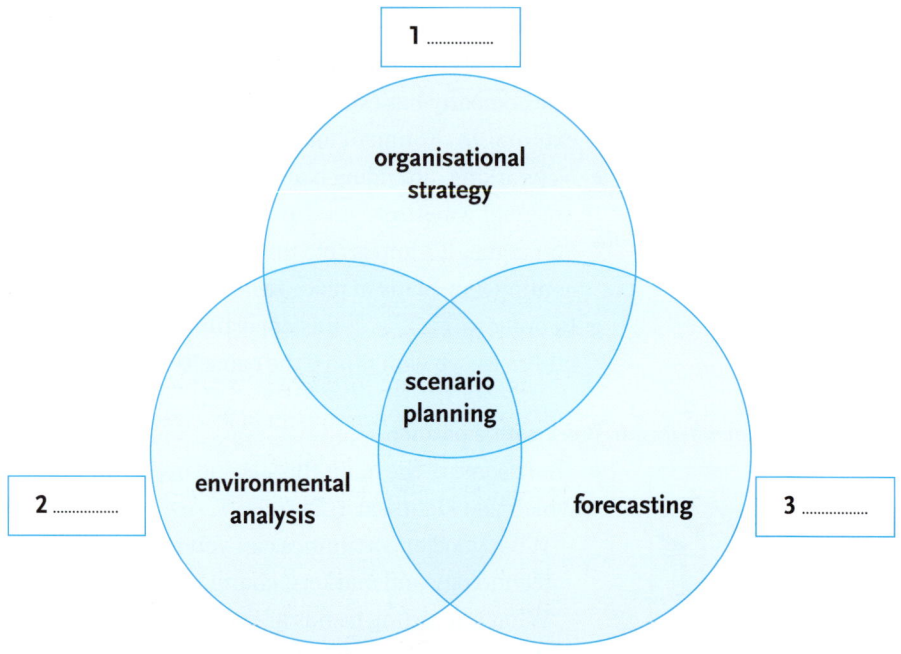

5 Look at these three examples from the dialogue. Which skill from Exercise 4 is Jon referring to each case?
   a There just aren't enough projects to guarantee future growth.
   b We've seen reductions in all of our European markets. Governments and commercial property investors have cut back.
   c I'm certain that this merger will ensure a secure future for us. If we want to get bigger projects, it's essential that we're part of a global group.

Focus on language

6 Complete the extracts below from Track 7 with the expressions in the box.

> it's essential have you considered let's consider what if
> I'm certain are likely we'd probably

a We've come together to examine some alternative scenarios. .... the first possibility.
b .... we merged with a larger organisation, like AKA? What would be the risks and opportunities?
c I'm sure we'll grow. However, ... lose control over the company direction.
d .... that they might get rid of you as soon as the merger's complete?
e Furthermore, our employees .... to object.
f I can see the potential risks you've outlined, Liliana. Nevertheless, ... that this merger will ensure a secure future for us.
g If we want to get bigger projects, ... that we're part of a global group.

7 Complete this table with two more expressions from Exercise 6 which express certainty and two more which suggest possibility.

certainty	possibility
it's essential	what if …?

8 Part of the challenge of communicating a change strategy is dealing with objections that may arise. These sentences are typical objections which may be made to a proposed change. Match one of the responses below from a manager (a–f) to each objection (1–6).

1 We've always done it like this.
2 I've been here for 30 years. I can't deal with all this.
3 We've heard it all before.
4 Why should we bother?
5 It sounds wonderful, but how can you be so sure that it will work?
6 It's too dangerous.

a We've measured the risks and we think that the risks of not changing are greater.
b But this time the plan hasn't just come from management. It's come from everybody agreeing about this together.
c The world is changing so fast that we simply can't go on doing things in the same old way any longer.
d Tell me how I can help you do it the new way. You're never too old to learn!
e The simple answer is that if we don't adapt, we won't survive.
f Of course we can't offer any guarantees. But if we all want it to work, it will.

9 Do you think the manager's responses in Exercise 8 are the best ones to give?

10 What other typical objections to change do we often hear? Can you think of other possible responses to these objections?

Let's talk

11 Read the situation on page 88. Imagine you are scenario planning in order to define a change strategy. Work in two groups, then present your results to the other group.
Group 1: What risks and opportunities do you see?
Group 2: If you went ahead with this idea, what objections might your employees have? What responses could you give to their objections?

C Professional skills: Making the case for change

Think about it
1 Can you give any examples from recent business history of large companies that have failed to see the future?

2 What do you know about Kodak and its products?

Read this
3 Read this article, then answer the questions on page 23.

The rise and fall of Kodak – what went wrong?

by Dr Steven McCabe

Kodak's announcement that it was filing for Chapter 11 protection bankruptcy protection brings to an end over 130 years of a brand that our grandparents' generation would have seen as revolutionising their lives.

Our children have grown up in a digital age where everything is instant. To those who lived at the end of the nineteenth century, merely seeing an image was like seeing magic being performed.

Kodak provided the technology to make this magic commonplace. The company that George Eastman started over 130 years ago was to become part of the lives of everyone who wanted to take pictures of events, both special and mundane.

Indeed, the fact that it also sold the film – its Kodachrome was accepted as the best available – meant that Kodak grew to a position that made it unassailable.

In 1976 in America, Kodak accounted for 90% of film and 85% of camera sales. Kodak was a brand that was both profitable and enjoyed high levels of sentiment from customers. What could go wrong?

With the benefit of hindsight, Kodak should have realised that digital cameras would be a threat to the 'cash cow' of the film and cameras they sold. As Kodak had developed a prototype of the digital camera in 1975, that should have meant it was well placed to cope with a phenomenon known as 'disruptive innovation'.

However, even though Kodak's research boffins had insights into what the future held for traditional cameras and films, most of its executives did not share their view. We can see that this was a classic case of hubris by executives who preferred to enjoy existing success rather than contemplating innovative developments that would represent a 'cannibalisation of film'.

The seminal book by Clayton Christensen, *The Innovator's Dilemma* (1997), recognises that Kodak faced significant problems. As he accepts, the challenges that Kodak faced in the late 1970s were so 'fundamentally different' to what it knew that perhaps it was simply better to 'kick the problem down the road' for others to worry about.

So what do we learn? Firstly, that no matter how good your brand is, it can never be 'future-proof'. Kodak is not the first and will certainly not be the last to make the mistake of misinterpreting the market. Customers are fickle and will alter their allegiance, given sufficient incentive.

Secondly, the world is turbulent. There is a need to constantly innovate and develop ideas which, of course, have no guarantee of success. Whilst it's tempting to wait until others have tried and then simply imitate, that is a dangerous strategy; it may then be too late.

Thirdly, organisations need to become more agile, which requires flexibility and the ability to cope with constant change and fluctuation. Achieving organisational agility is not easy if decision-making is centralised and people are expected to follow top-down instructions. It is critical to encourage your people to search for new ideas and solutions to existing problems. They may be closer to the customers than senior executives can ever hope to be.

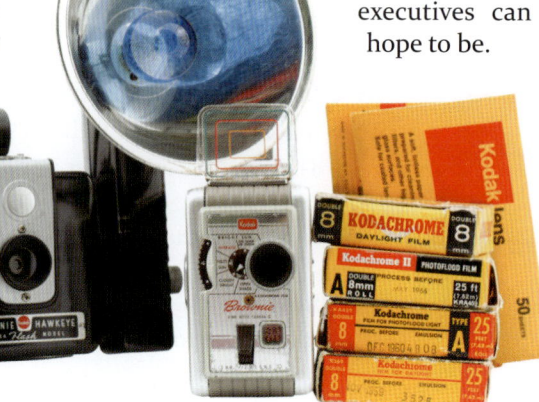

adapted from The Birmingham Post Business blog

a When, according to the article, was Kodak at its height?
b What did it fail to see coming?
c What do you think is meant by *disruptive innovation*?
d What do you think is meant by a *cannibalisation of film*?
e What, according to the author, are the three lessons to be learned from the Kodak case?

4 What steps should an organisation take to ensure that it is ready to face the future?

Focus on language

5 Match each of these words and phrases from the text (1–8) with its definition (a–h).

1	hindsight	a	too much pride
2	cash cow	b	often changing
3	boffins	c	fast-moving
4	hubris	d	knowing now what we didn't know then
5	fickle	e	research scientists
6	allegiance	f	unpredictable
7	turbulent	g	a very profitable part of the business
8	agile	h	loyalty

> You can use *should have* + past participle to talk about lessons learned from past experience. Look at these two examples from the text:
> With the benefit of hindsight, Kodak **should have realised** that digital cameras would be a threat to the 'cash cow' of the film and cameras they sold.
> As Kodak had developed a prototype of the digital camera in 1975, that **should have meant** it was well placed to cope with a phenomenon known as 'disruptive innovation'.

6 Look at some of the reasons why several large companies have failed since 2008. Rewrite the sentences using the prompts and *should have* or *shouldn't have*. Remember to use the past participle of the verb.

a Kodak didn't commercialise digital camera technology.
Kodak / develop / digital cameras / in the 1980s
Kodak should have developed digital cameras in the 1980s.

b Borders had too many large stores and lost business to a successful online retailer.
Borders / reduce / the number and size of stores / and / invest / more / in / an online strategy

c Habitat produced innovative but expensive furniture and household goods, but lost market share to cheaper competitors in the 1990s.
Habitat / change / its business model / or / produce / cheaper products

d Hollywood Video didn't respond to a changing world where online movie streaming has taken over from traditional movie rental.
Hollywood video / invest / in / a video-streaming channel

e Lehman Brothers borrowed too much and made loans to people who couldn't pay the money back.
Lehman Brothers / borrow / so much / and / make / loans / to people who couldn't pay the money back

Let's talk

7 Discuss these questions with a partner.
a What should Kodak have done differently from the 1970s onwards?
b What other technologies have replaced traditional cameras?
c What do you think is the future of other common electronic products, e.g. TVs, desktop and laptop computers?
d Do you think mobile payments will replace credit cards and cash?
e What other opportunities could mobile or online technology open up in the future?

D Intercultural competence: Communicating a vision across cultures

1 Discuss these questions with a partner.
  a What kind of management style is encouraged in your organisation?
  b How did you 'learn' your management style? (on the job / on a company-specific development programme / at university)

2 Match each of these management styles (1–5) with its definition (a–e).
  1 strategic
  2 autocratic
  3 tactical
  4 participative
  5 paternalistic

  a Managing top down, giving orders and instructions
  b Senior managers having a responsibility to protect employees in exchange for loyalty
  c Making decisions based on situations as they arise, 'getting things done'
  d Analysing the internal and external environment, looking forward to set longer-term objectives
  e Delegating power, being inclusive and sharing decision-making

3 Match these comments from managers (a–e) with each different kind of management style in Exercise 2 (1–5).
  a 'I have examined all the factors associated with our customers and competitors, as well as our own strengths and weaknesses, and I have established some objectives for our longer-term direction.'
  b 'I know you've done a lot of analysis and you're thinking long term, but I think we should choose the best methods for each situation as it comes – we just can't predict what will happen.'
  c 'Our aim is to increase our market share by 5% this year, and this is how we're going to do it. Jan, you'll redesign the marketing plan for me to check. Bernhard, I want you to do a full competitor analysis and report to me on Monday.'
  d 'We need to improve the XY31, and I'd like you all to be involved. So let's brainstorm some ideas. Fred, could you start?'
  e 'I'm afraid we can't consider firing these employees. We have a responsibility to them and to their families.'

4 Discuss these questions.
  a Does your predominant management style fit any of the descriptions in Exercise 2?
  b How have you had to adapt your style in different contexts?
  c Have you ever had a manager who came from a different company or country with a very different management style? How did you learn to work successfully together?

5 Which style do you think would be most appropriate in these contexts, and why?
  a You are a leader on an oil rig and a serious security risk occurs. You need to get your team to act decisively and quickly.
  b You are leading a small entrepreneurial start-up technology company and you want your team to develop an innovative new product.
  c You manage a large factory with 250 operators in a rural region where you are the only employer. Your employees are reliable and hard-working, but the factory is threatened by cuts, and you need to negotiate with senior management to save jobs.
  d You are a middle manager in an international company. The ongoing financial crisis has caused the company to change its senior management and strategy several times in the past three years. Things are very uncertain, and you have to somehow both support the people and manage the business day to day.

Case study: Adapting a change strategy in China

> *... the business environment is less stable than it was, and it is, therefore, very possible that the Chinese style of business management, with its emphasis on vision and tactics, is better adapted to today's environment than the Western style, with its emphasis on strategy.*
>
> From *China's Management Revolution*
> by Charles Edouard Bouée

Background Netwerks is a global company based in Berlin, Germany, which sells networking and communication technology. Five years ago, Netwerks saw an opportunity to be more competitive by producing its equipment in China, so it entered into a joint venture with a local company making similar products. This proved to be a successful strategy, and the Chinese business has developed into a whole business unit, including a sales distribution arm. Now Netwerks faces a new threat from smaller competitors. Although they can't compete on price, they are far more innovative than Netwerks and are gaining market share rapidly.

As a result, a new plan for innovation and change has been developed by senior management. The new vision is to:
- sell flexible, innovative products to large organisations and governments
- be the most trusted and secure networking and communications supplier globally
- provide the fastest, most responsive service.

The task now is to translate this vision into reality in each global region.

Situation Fred Narib, a product manager, has been chosen to go to China to take over as the liaison officer with the local business unit. His task is to work with the Chinese team to develop a strategy to implement the global vision locally. He is an expert in the field of computer technology and is a rising young star in the company. He is a goal-driven, energetic, direct communicator. He is quite strategic in his thinking and he also has a participative management style, which has worked well with the teams he's managed in the past.

🎧 **8** Fred had a meeting with the local team – Shen, Mr Zhèng (a senior manager) and Mr Luó (the chairman) – to present the new vision. Listen to Fred's proposal and look at these responses.

Shen
> Um, well, I'm not sure really, but it looks very interesting …

Mr Zhèng
> We believe it's very important to preserve our quality and reliability. The other points we will discuss.

Mr Luó
> Excuse me, but we will have to adjourn the meeting.

After some private discussions, the team came back to him the next day and told him that they cannot accept most of his proposals.

Task You are members of the China liaison team at the Berlin office. Fred is now very confused and calls you to ask for some guidance.

1 Read the cultural briefing information on page 88.

2 Consider these questions and agree on the advice that you should give Fred.
   a Who should Fred talk to first about his proposals?
   b Are there any common points of agreement which could be built on?
   c How could decisions be made in this context?
   d What should Fred have done differently? How could he adapt his approach in future?

E Language reference

Read through the key words and phrases below. Add any other useful words and expressions which you feel are important for you to learn. Make sure you find the time to review these words and phrases regularly and to use them at work.

Threats
growing Asian competition
high prices
low sales
ineffective marketing
underinvestment
exposure to debt

Opportunities
great products
CAM (computer-aided manufacturing)
developing new skills
online purchasing
new technology

Verbs to use with *threat/opportunity*
face / identify / ignore / confront **a threat**
look for / ignore / miss / exploit / use **an opportunity**

Scenario planning
certainty: I'm sure, I'm certain, it's essential
possibility: What if …?, we'd probably, Have you considered … might …?, are likely

Dealing with objections
This plan has come from everyone agreeing about it together.
We can't go on doing things in the same old way.
How can I help you do it in the new way?
You're never too old to learn!
We can't offer any guarantees, but if we all want it to work, it will work.

Lessons learned
What should we have done differently?
We should have invested in an online strategy.
We shouldn't have borrowed so much money.

Management styles
autocratic
participative
paternalistic
strategic
tactical

Writing task You are a senior sales and marketing professional for a café and sandwich chain. You make healthy sandwiches and salads, coffee, etc. to order in your city-centre outlets for the business-lunch market. You have recently read an article about mobile ordering and payment technology. You think that your company should be investing in this. Your argument is that business people are extremely busy, with less and less time for lunch. The customer would benefit from placing and paying for their order from their smartphone to pick up from a designated outlet or, alternatively, group orders could be placed for delivery to offices. You know that this will involve financial investment, and economic times are hard. However, you have noticed sales dropping and customers walking out because they don't have time to wait. You feel it's urgent to do something to change. Write an e-mail to your boss outlining your proposal and arguing the case for change.

F Change-management working tips and personal action plan

1 Take a few minutes to reflect on these tips on managing change which arise from this unit. How far do you agree with each one? Which do you think is the most important, and which ideas are the most useful?

TIP 1
Think about the changes that have gone on around you and why they have happened. What are the trends in your industry, and what do you think your business needs to do to remain relevant going forward?
Ideas for analysing changes:
- Listen to the opinions and ideas of diverse groups of managers and executives, as well as external partners, in order to analyse scenarios that might not normally be considered. This may change your standard view of the world.
- Start to visualise all the possible futures, as this helps you to see why change is necessary and pushes you to develop actions.

TIP 2
Change may be necessary because developments in technology and consumer preferences overtake a company's products or services. However, there will always be people who object to the idea of change, especially if they don't believe there is a real need, due to past or present success.
Ideas for overcoming opposition to change:
- Plan for all possible objections and prepare a convincing case based on analysis and research for why your company needs to change.
- Give examples of companies that failed to change and the consequences.
- Ask questions to encourage people to examine the validity of their own objections.

TIP 3
Many managers develop a predominant management style based on what is accepted and works well in their national and organisational culture. Some companies develop their own very strong and distinctive leadership approach. However, it has become more important to develop a range of styles of leadership which can be drawn on, depending on the context.
Ideas for linking management style and change:
- Try to identify what your predominant leadership style is and think about in which contexts it works well. Then, imagine a series of scenarios in which it might not work as well.
- Be adaptable and lead in the right way for the context. Keep a record of your successes and failures, and note how other leaders act in different circumstances.

Personal action plan 2 Take 15 minutes to review the unit. Write down at least three important points that you have learned and that you want to apply to your change-management practice. Then commit to a schedule to implement your learning and think about how you can check if you have been successful.

	what I have learned and want to apply in my change-management practice	when/how I will apply this in my change-management practice	how I will check if I have applied it
1			
2			
3			

3 Communicating change

AIMS
A To communicate change effectively
B To use the right language
C To communicate clearly in a crisis
D To develop flexibility in communication style

A Discussion and listening

Think about it

> *The less people know, the more they yell.*
> Seth Godin (1960–),
> American entrepreneur,
> author and public speaker

1 When implementing change at work, what different things do you have to communicate?
Example: Presenting the case for change, ...

2 Think about a change process you have been involved in. How was it communicated?
- **top down** (Senior management decided what would happen and told you about it.)
- **collaboratively** (Senior management told you there was a need for change and invited you to contribute ideas and solutions.)
- **delegated** (Senior management told you what the company needed to achieve and asked you to decide what needed to change and how to implement solutions to reach company goals.)

Listen to this

3 You are going to listen to three people talking about major change programmes. Listen to each one and answer the questions that follow.

🎧 **9** Adriano Moura works in the finance department of a nationwide transport company in Rio de Janeiro, Brazil.
a How was change communicated – top down, collaboratively or delegated?
b Why does Adriano have such a negative view of change?
c What was the most important thing Adriano felt his boss could have done differently during the last change process?

🎧 **10** Sanjay Prasanna is a software engineer working for a rapidly growing IT company in Bangalore, India.
d How was change communicated – top down, collaboratively or delegated?
e What does Sanjay mean when he says that his boss is the 'eyes and ears of the organisation'?
f Why do you think Sanjay is not afraid of change?

🎧 **11** Erika Schmidt is a human resources manager in a large engineering company in Stuttgart, Germany.
g How was change communicated – top down, collaboratively or delegated?
h Why does Erika think the previous change programmes she experienced in her company were not that effective?
i According to Erika, what was different about the change process introduced by the new Swedish CEO?

Focus on language

4 **Complete the gaps in the text below with the verbs from the box.**

| agree | ask | come up with | engage | invite |
| involve | listen | take part | talk | tell |

Successful communication is a two-way process, and this is especially true when communicating change. You can **(a)** .... people about your vision in a presentation, and you can **(b)** .... about it at a big conference, but if you don't **(c)** .... people from the beginning, they will not **(d)** .... with the process of change. Why not **(e)** .... all the people who will be affected by the change to **(f)** .... in an open discussion? **(g)** .... them to **(h)** .... ideas and then **(i)** .... what needs to change and how to do it. Most importantly, **(j)** .... to people. You may think it takes too much time, but in the long term, you'll probably find that your change process will be more successful.

5 **Read the comments below from the interviews in Exercise 3. Match each one (a–f) with a heading from the box (1–6).**

> 1 Preserving key benefits
> 2 Being treated fairly
> 3 Being given responsibility for change
> 4 Having the opportunity to express opinions
> 5 Having a good relationship with management
> 6 Having competence recognised

a If something is going to change, and we have a grievance, we want to know that we can speak openly and not suffer consequences

b We just feel we've been trusted to make the changes we feel are necessary in the way we think best.

c I don't have to be a part of every change decision, but if I don't like something, I want to be listened to.

d We know our area and our people better than anybody, and we feel this has been recognised.

e Recently, our boss saw a problem was coming, so he invited us to a meeting and presented the situation. Then he said, 'Tell me, what shall we do about it?' Together, we came up with solutions and agreed what we could change and what we wanted to keep – like our healthcare, for example.

f We feel like our boss is our friend, and the company helps us and our families. It's important that we have a harmonious relationship with our employer.

Let's talk

6 **When things change, what can managers say and do to show that they trust, listen to and recognise employees' points of view? In small groups, draw up a list of 'change communication' guidelines, then present them to the other groups.**

3 Communicating change

B Communication skills: Using the right language

Think about it

> When we communicate change, we sometimes need to **push** (give a strong message, tell people what decisions have been made and what they need to do, convince people of the urgency of a situation, push to meet targets and deadlines) and sometimes we need to **pull** (ask people what they think, elicit ideas and opinions, share decision-making, delegate goal-setting and achievement of targets).

1 Discuss these questions in groups.
   a How much of your time do you spend telling people to do things, and how much do you spend asking them?
   b Do you think you have the balance right between a push (telling) and a pull (asking) style of communication?
   c Can you think of a time when it was important to push and another when it was important to pull? In both cases, what was the outcome?

Listen to this

2 🎧 **12** Albert Capper is the owner and managing director of Photoprint, a family company based in Manchester in the UK. He is concerned about the future of the company and has called a meeting with his key managers – Param, Gail and Yoko – to talk about the problems the business faces. Listen to the discussion and answer these questions.
   a How does Albert start the discussion? Does his communication style rely more on pushing (telling) or pulling (asking)?
   b What does Yoko think should happen?
   c How does Albert bring the first part of the meeting to a close?
   d What is the key message Albert wants to communicate to staff?

3 🎧 **13** Listen to a subsequent discussion between Param, Gail and Yoko and answer these questions.
   a What does Param believe they need to do to achieve their targets?
   b What is Yoko's opinion about the proposal from the other managers?
   c Do you think Yoko favours a push or a pull approach? Why?

4 When a company is in trouble, is it better to be more optimistic and communicate positive messages for as long as possible, or to be pessimistic and talk about problems sooner rather than later? In this context, is it better to push or pull?

Focus on language

5 Look at these examples of 'involving' language taken from Tracks 12 and 13 and write them in the corresponding rows of the table on the next page.
Our loyal workforce has been the key to our success up to now.
~~I'd like to hear your views on what we can do to change.~~
Where should we be going in the next three years?
Thanks, Yoko. I agree that it's important to be open and honest with staff …
What can we do to change and survive?
Can't we retrain people for different jobs?
We could also use selected photos to produce professional videos with music …
Let's summarise and agree what we're going to communicate.
So, you're saying that … people can be home-based …
Thanks for your contributions, you're a great team.
I'll produce a proposal for the May 15th meeting.

asking for opinions	I'd like to hear your views on what we can do to change.
showing you're listening	
committing to action	
suggesting ideas	
recognising value	
pushing communication to a close	

> When we are involved in discussions about change, we also need to:
> - talk about possible futures
> - talk about things we are convinced about
> - agree to do or not do something
> - talk about consequences.

6 Look at these examples from Track 13 and match each use of *will* with one of the functions from the box above.

   a If we do this, I'm sure we **will** get the results we need.
   b I**'ll** outline the services we can offer with budget and technical requirements.
   c My biggest concern is that whilst we're talking and asking and retraining and all that, we**'ll** run out of money.
   d We need to be clear and tell staff that unless we cut stores and jobs first, we **won't** be in a position to restructure …

7 Complete these statements in as many ways as you can.

   a In three years, my company will probably be producing/offering ....
   b I'm sure that I'll .... next year.
   c I've promised my boss that I'll .... However, I won't be able to ....
   d Unless the global economic situation improves, ... won't ....

Let's talk **8** Work with a partner. You are going to take the roles of a manager and one of their team members. Following a change in their role, the manager has asked for a meeting with the team member to discuss the impact of this change. Practise exercising good communication skills in a changing work environment.

   Student A: See below.   Student B: Turn to page 92.

> **Student A**
> You are Student B's manager. They are a good employee, but have not had very long in their current job and need quite a lot of support, so you also act as coach and mentor. So far, you have worked in the same office and have had a good working relationship. However, you are now being promoted to manage more people and you are also going to move to another office on the other side of the city, so you will have less time to support Student B than in the past. Have a meeting with Student B in which you give them the news of the change and come to an agreement about how you are going to work together in the future. Think about how you can:
> - ask for opinions
> - show you are listening
> - commit to action
> - suggest ideas
> - recognise value
> - push communication to a close.

3 Communicating change

C Professional skills: Communicating clearly in a crisis

Think about it 1 Have you ever had to communicate in a crisis, or have you been at the receiving end of communication in such a situation? What styles and channels of communication are generally used in this context, and why?

2 What do you remember about the collapse of the financial firm Lehman Brothers?

Read this 3 Read this article, then answer the questions below.

Wall Street crisis: Lehman staff tell their stories

1 An internal communication was handed out to members of staff as they entered the building at Canary Wharf this morning. It read: 'Our e-mail earlier today provided high-level information regarding recent changes impacting the firm. We will update you as soon as possible on these developments and their impact on the UK business. In the interim, it is important that we do not commit any financial obligations to third parties until the situation is clearer. Accordingly, no trades or other transactions may be entered into by members of staff today without prior clearance from a member of the Europe and Middle East operating committee. We realise this will contribute to the uncertainty in the short term, but this is a necessary precaution to protect your interests and those of the firm.'

2 The collapse of Lehman Brothers, which has lost billions of dollars on risky mortgage-backed investments, followed the failure of rescue talks over the weekend. Its US parent subsequently filed for bankruptcy protection in America early today, with administrators being called into its European headquarters in London hours later. Today, Duo Ai, 26, who worked in Research, said the atmosphere inside the building at Canary Wharf was one of shock. He said: 'A lot of people are very sad. I heard someone was crying. I guess it's understandable if they invested a lot in Lehman stock. We really didn't see this coming. On Friday, we were still holding out hope that some bank would buy Lehman. Everyone's understanding is that everyone is gone and everyone is clearing their desks. I couldn't sleep last night but stayed up talking about what was going to happen. The only question that remains is whether we will get this month's pay cheque.'

3 John Collins, 40, who works in Equity Derivatives Product Control, said he had been told not to come back tomorrow. 'People are trying to put a brave face on it, but obviously there are some disconsolate people in there who have taken it very badly,' he said. 'They say the economy is in its worst position since the 1920s. And they could be right. It's only the guys at the top who really know what's happening.'

4 In New York, Lehman workers also complained about lack of information. 'We're not trading and we're just kind of waiting to hear,' said one worker in Fixed Income. 'We have gone straight to acceptance. We have gone through the stages of grief – there is not much you can do about it. People are getting their résumés together, but it is not the best time to be looking for a job in financial services. But you do what you have to do. It was quick. It surprised me. But that is the pace of finance these days. Things can go that quickly, they are so very highly leveraged.'

adapted from www.guardian.co.uk

a How were members of staff in the UK initially informed about changes that had affected the company?
b What was the main objective of the message given to UK members of staff?
c Why did Lehman Brothers ultimately collapse?
d According to Duo Ai, why were employees so stunned by the collapse?
e According to John Collins, who did know about the state of the bank?
f What did the employees in New York know about the status of their jobs?
g According to the employee in New York, what is particularly shocking about change in the financial sector?

4 Why do you think Lehman Brothers communicated with its staff in the way it did? Do you think that, in the circumstances, there was a better way?

Focus on language

5 Find words/phrases in paragraph 1 which match these definitions.
   a a message restricted to members of an organisation
   b distributed
   c facts coming from top management
   d keep informed about progress
   e when no one knows what is happening

6 Find words/phrases in paragraphs 2–4 which match these definitions.
   a the feeling around a place
   b disbelief
   c It was unexpected.
   d being optimistic
   e what people know
   f very unhappy
   g coming to terms with what has happened

7 When conveying a message, it is useful to answer these questions:
   1 What is the key message?
   2 Why? What is the problem?
   3 What does this mean?
   4 What outcome/solution do we want?

   Match each answer below (a–d) from the internal communication to Lehman Brothers employees with a question above (1–4).
   a recent changes impacting the firm
   b to protect your interests and those of the firm
   c … no trades or other transactions may be entered into by members of staff today without prior clearance from a member of the Europe and Middle East operating committee.
   d It is important that we do not commit any financial obligations to third parties …

8 Imagine that you have to communicate the message from Exercise 7 by video conference to a large number of employees. Complete the announcement below using the phrases from the box.

This is due to	The purpose of this	We are doing this to	This means that

   (a) .... announcement is to tell you it is important that we do not commit any financial obligations to third parties. (b) .... recent changes impacting the firm. (c) .... no trades or other transactions may be entered into by members of staff today without prior clearance from a member of the Europe and Middle East operating committee. (d) .... protect your interests and those of the firm.

Let's talk

9 Ask a partner to think of a message they need to communicate to their team. Ask them the questions from Exercise 7 to get the required information. If you can't think of a message of your own, one of you can ask the questions and the other can use the information on page 89 as an example. When you have all the information you need, present your partner's message to the group using the phrases from Exercise 8 to introduce each point.

'What if – and I know this sounds kooky – we communicated with the employees?'

3 Communicating change

D Intercultural competence: Developing flexibility in communication style

1 Think about the people you work with, for example your local team. What differences are there in the way people communicate? For example, are some more dominant, some more reserved? Do some people pull more and some push more?

2 Have you ever done a personality profile which told you something about your communication style? If yes, how useful was the exercise, and how did you use the results? If no, ask someone in the group who has experience to tell you about it.

> When communicating internationally, it is often necessary to adapt your communication style to better match the styles of your partners. In order to do this, it is helpful to understand your own style in more detail.

3 a Do this short questionnaire.

1 In a meeting, I usually prefer to:
 a listen carefully to what others are saying.
 b ask plenty of questions to explore opinions.
 c give my opinion early in the discussion.

2 If I disagree with something said in a meeting, I usually:
 a keep my thoughts to myself.
 b see if others agree with me.
 c say clearly why I disagree.

3 When I walk into a room full of strangers, I usually:
 a go up to anyone I see and start talking straight away.
 b spend a little time working up the courage to talk to someone.
 c stand apart and drink my coffee on my own.

4 In social conversations, I usually:
 a listen more than speak.
 b speak more than listen.
 c do about the same amount of speaking and listening.

5 The way I communicate is:
 a very direct.
 b quite direct.
 c rather indirect.

6 As a listener, I am:
 a very active – I always signal (by nodding and smiling) that I am listening.
 b moderately active – I sometimes signal that I am listening.
 c rather silent – I don't give much sign that I am listening.

7 When I speak, I am usually:
 a very structured and organised.
 b moderately structured and organised.
 c quite spontaneous and not very structured.

8 When dealing with new people, I am usually quite:
 a task-focused – I don't need to get to know the people I am dealing with.
 b people-focused – I do need to get to know the people I am dealing with.
 c balanced between task and people focus.

b Work with a partner whose communication style you know.
- Say what you think their answers are.
- Listen to what they think is your communication style.
- Discuss how similar or different from each other your styles are.
- Decide on one point you would like to change.

Case study: Communicating change across borders

Background A virtual team is one where most, if not all, of the communication among team members is done remotely rather than face to face – by e-mail, phone call, telephone conference, video conference, etc. Dubai Eastward is an investment company working mainly in the Middle East and Asia, with different departmental teams working virtually. The human resources team is composed of four country managers working in Dubai (the team leader), Mumbai, Shanghai and Sydney.

Situation Due to a big fall in profits in the company last year, senior management have decided to implement a new system of internal controls globally. This will mean:
- a reduction of 20% in each individual's budget
- more detailed reporting of activity and expenditure on a monthly basis
- weekly reporting by phone to the team leader
- a prioritisation of activities.

There is going to be a meeting in which the team leader will explain why the new system needs to be implemented. The country managers will have the opportunity to ask questions and get clarification on details, but can also present their ideas, especially on what cuts they could make in their country and how they will make time for the new procedures.

Task 1 Form groups of four to role-play the meeting.
Student A: See below.
Student B: Turn to page 92.
Student C: Turn to page 94.
Student D: Turn to page 95.

Student A
You are the leader of the HR team based in Dubai and you are also the Dubai country manager. Your job is to communicate the need for the other three country managers to accept and implement the four changes required by senior management. Make sure that you are clear how each one intends to proceed. Ask them what support they need.

---

2 When you have finished the role-play:
a provide feedback to each other on the process and outcomes of the meeting
b discuss the challenges of communicating change with a culturally diverse and geographically dispersed group of people.

E Language reference

Read through the key words and phrases below. Add any other useful words and expressions which you feel are important for you to learn. Make sure you find the time to review these words and phrases regularly and to use them at work.

Management
be powerful	be a guide and mentor
trust and respect employees	set the limits
be honest	be the eyes and ears of the organisation

Employees
take part in the process
have a grievance
speak openly
be listened to
come up with solutions together
have a harmonious relationship with employer
feel engaged/involved/trusted

Verbs for communicating change
tell	come up with
take part	agree
listen	involve
talk	ask
invite	engage

Involving language
I'd like to hear your views on …	What can we do?
Where should we be going?	So you're saying …

Making suggestions
Can't we …?
We could …
Let's …

Closing
Let's summarise and agree …

Committing to action
I'll produce a proposal.
I'll outline the services we can offer.

Expressing formality
It is important that we …	We will update you as soon as possible on …
This is a necessary precaution.	Accordingly, …
We realise that …	In the interim, …

Constructing a message
The purpose of this is …	This means that …
This is due to …	We are doing this to …

Writing task Look again at the situation relating to Section C, Exercise 9 (page 89). Following the meeting with the managers, you have agreed to these points.
- Complete a full safety review on all company oil tankers within six weeks.
- Request that all members of engineering teams work overtime, with no holidays to be taken during this period.
- Team to familiarise themselves with new maintenance procedures and complete the essential safety review within the timeframe.
- Repeat safety checks annually, not every five years as before.
- Priority is to repair damage to company reputation and avoid future accidents and losses.

Write an e-mail to the engineering team members to clearly communicate this message.

F Change-management working tips and personal action plan

1 Take a few minutes to reflect on these tips on managing change which arise from this unit. How far do you agree with each one? Which do you think is the most important, and which ideas are the most useful?

TIP 1

You can communicate change top-down; you can invite employees to collaborate with management to develop a plan for change; or you can set goals and delegate actions.
Ideas for deciding how to communicate change:
- Give responsibility for transformation to the people it impacts, as this is usually more successful. Break your change strategy into steps and delegate each area to the relevant people.
- Use social-media channels, e-mail, video conferences and open meetings as communication channels between management and employees.
- Focus on the big picture and track the impact of the change effort on the organisation as a whole.

TIP 2

In some cases, there isn't time for collaboration, delegation or a lot of discussion. When you have to communicate a message urgently or in a crisis, the most important thing is to be very clear and to communicate as much information as you can.
Ideas for communicating in a crisis:
- People really need to know what is happening, why it's happening, what this means for them as individuals and what the outcome will be. Make sure your message answers the key questions in people's minds.
- If you can't give all the information, make sure you explain why, when more information will be available and how people can access information. Focus particularly on what the change 'means for them' and finally allow plenty of time to answer questions and address individual concerns.

TIP 3

There is no one communication style that is appropriate for every context. The key is to develop a range of styles and to increase your awareness of the impact your communication has on other people.
Ideas for adapting communication style:
- Ask questions, ask people for their opinion, recognise the value of people's contributions and show you're listening by summarising and clarifying.
- Translate employees' ideas into actions.
- Communicate messages clearly, give people information and push for decisions.
- In different cultural settings, observe how people communicate, who communicates what and get feedback on your communication style.

Personal action plan 2 Take 15 minutes to review the unit. Write down at least three important points that you have learned and that you want to apply to your change-management practice. Then commit to a schedule to implement your learning and think about how you can check if you have been successful.

	what I have learned and want to apply in my change-management practice	when/how I will apply this in my change-management practice	how I will check if I have applied it
1			
2			
3			

3 Communicating change

4 Overcoming resistance

AIMS
A To identify why people resist change
B To deal with resistance
C To deal with the consequences of redundancies
D To understand motivation across cultures

A Discussion and listening

Think about it

> *Difficulties strengthen the mind, as labour does the body.*
> Lucius Annaeus Seneca (5BC–65AD),
> Roman poet

1 Discuss these questions with a partner.
a What are some of the reasons why people resist change?
b When faced with change, what concerns you most? What do you fear losing?
c What can you as a manager do to help your team members adapt to change?

Listen to this

2 🎧 **14** The Italian dairy company Emilanolat has decided to merge with a larger German food company. The board of the German company is particularly interested in Emilanolat's ice-cream range. Talal Malouf is an interim manager who has been appointed to facilitate the integration process. Listen to him talking about Marco, one of the people involved in the merger, and answer these questions.
a What was Marco afraid of losing as a result of the merger?
b Why did Talal feel it was important to gain Marco's support in the change process?
c How did Talal get Marco to support the new organisation?

3 🎧 **15** Listen to Talal discussing Helmut and answer these questions.
a How did Helmut's position change following the merger?
b What three steps were taken to deal with Helmut's reaction to the changes?

Focus on language

4 One factor in change situations is the ability to influence others. Complete each of these sentences with the correct form of the word *influence*. The first three examples come from Track 14.
a The first job is to identify the .... in the organisation, the key people who need to be brought into the process somehow.
b In fact, he still had a lot of .... over the whole department. He was very loyal ...
c It's always advisable to listen to .... people and negotiate with them if you can. In this way, you get their support and the support of others.
d Marco .... his team, because he supported them and represented their interests during the merger.
e It's important to develop a range of communication styles in order to .... different kinds of people effectively.
f Organisations can be very political. This means that you can gain .... by building relationships with key people.

5 When people resist change, it's a leader's job to help them to adapt. Complete each of these sentences with the correct form of *resist* or *adapt*. The first two examples come from Track 15.
  a Initially, some people agreed with him, but in time, most of the team .... to the changes and got on with the job to be done.
  b We started by having a series of one-to-one discussions, to listen to his grievances and to look for ways to help him ....
  c Helmut reacted by .... the changes and by trying to influence others.
  d Common reasons why people .... change are: loss of power and position, fear of uncertainty, and a mismatch of values and beliefs.
  e Listening to people in a series of individual and group meetings can help reduce ....

6 Complete the extracts below with an appropriate preposition from the box.

| behind | for | into | on | through | to |

  a The first job is to identify the 'influencers' in the organisation, the key people who need to be brought .... the process somehow.
  b He was very loyal, and the way he represented his people's position meant that they all stood .... him.
  c We asked Marco what we could exchange .... his support.
  d Helmut became increasingly opposed .... the changes.
  e All employees are given time to work .... their anger and frustration.
  f There comes a point where people have to move .... to the next phase – acceptance.

7 The phrases below can be used in interviews with staff to show that you are listening and helping them to adapt to change. Complete each one with an appropriate preposition from the box.

| about | about | through | to | with |

  a I have heard that some staff do not agree .... the changes. How do you feel .... this?
  b I understand that you are not happy .... the change in your role. Is that correct?
  c How can I help you adjust .... this change?
  d What can I do to help you get .... this transition period?

Let's talk **8** Work with a partner. Your company is based in Germany. The management has decided to streamline and move some of its HR and finance functions to other locations.
Student A: See below.
Student B: Turn to page 92.

> **Student A**
> You are a manager in the finance department, based in Germany. None of your team will lose their job as a result of the reorganisation, but work locations, roles and responsibilities will change. One member of your team seems unhappy. You decide to phone them to discuss the situation.
> At this stage, you should:
> - show you want to listen
> - establish what the employee is opposed to, note down all the issues and summarise at the end to make sure you have understood everything
> - arrange a follow-up meeting with the team member to begin the process of moving from resistance to acceptance.

4 Overcoming resistance

B Communication skills: Dealing with resistance

Think about it

> **Coaching**: a one-to-one relationship where one person helps the other (usually by asking questions, not advising or telling) to identify an issue, focus on solutions, and achieve goals.

1 Look at the definition of coaching above. Have you ever tried coaching somebody, or have you ever been coached? What was your experience?

2 Coaching is one way to help people overcome resistance to change. Think about a context you are facing where someone is unhappy about a change. Do you think coaching could be a helpful tool for you to use? Why? / Why not?

Listen to this

3 🎧 **16** Bamberg is a video-conferencing equipment company which has recently been acquired by FW Net, a large IT networking firm. FW Net is in the process of integrating Bamberg's staff, systems and processes. The first task is for Bamberg employees to familiarise themselves with the new systems and ways of working. Jean Milieu is a departmental manager from FW Net. He has been asked to talk to one of his Bamberg team members, Rui Silveira, who still isn't connected to the FW Net system. Jean and Rui have exchanged e-mails about the problems Rui is experiencing, and they have now arranged a phone call to talk through the issues. Listen to the first part of the call and answer these questions.
   a What is the purpose of the call?
   b Which issue is identified as the priority?

4 🎧 **17** Listen to the second part of the call and answer these questions.
   a Why is Rui unclear about what he should do?
   b What does Rui decide he could do to clarify his role?
   c How is Rui going to measure his success?
   d What difference is there between the way FW Net works and the way Bamberg worked?
   e What do you think of Jean's approach? Do you think this sort of approach can be effective when helping people adapt to change?

My coffee was just a little bit too hot this morning, Tom.

Great coaching is about being specific with feedback.

www.CartoonStock.com

Focus on language

5 Complete the questions below from Tracks 16 and 17 with the phrases from the box.

how could you	how will you know	shall we
what could stop you	what have you done so far	what are you going to do
what exactly	can you prioritise	

   a .... what you see as the main problem?
   b .... is stopping you from doing your job well?
   c Right, so what you're saying is you're not clear about your role? .... focus on that today?
   d .... to establish your role and responsibilities?
   e .... clarify what you and others should be doing?
   f .... from achieving your goals?
   g Could you just go through what we've talked about? .... , by when …
   h … and .... if you've been successful?

6 Match the phrases from the discussion between Rui and Jean (a–g) with what is the speaker trying to do in each case (1–7).

1 showing empathy
2 stating a purpose
3 recognising value
4 intervening in a conversation
5 clarifying a point
6 reassuring
7 making a suggestion

a As I said in my e-mail, the reason I'm calling you today is to start helping you through the issues that you told me about.
b If I can recap, you said that you're not happy with the organisational changes and the new process that we've introduced.
c I'm sorry, Rui, could I just interrupt you for a moment?
d Let's try to break this problem into small steps.
e That sounds like a really good idea.
f I'd like you to know that I do understand your position.
g Don't worry, we're here to support you.

7 Management sometimes makes mistakes or fails to prepare the ground in advance when implementing change programmes; this gives people genuine reason to resist change. Match each of the statements below (a–h) with one of the issues from the box.

> bad timing   climate of mistrust   fear of failure
> fear of the unknown   lack of reward system   loss of status or job security
> organisational politics   protecting interests of own group

a These changes'll mean that my role and responsibilities will be reduced.
b I won't be rewarded or gain anything from supporting this change.
c This is a total surprise. I'd heard some rumours that we might merge with another organisation, but that's all. I don't like it when I'm not sure what's going on.
d I manage a team of 20 people – they've been loyal to me and the company for many years. This change means some of them might be forced to move location or lose their jobs. I can't let that happen!
e I don't trust the senior management because the last time we had a change programme, they told us our factory would be safe; a year later, it was closed and we were all moved to other sites.
f I have to say that I don't really agree with the decision to appoint this group of people to lead the change initiative. I don't think they're qualified to do it. There were better candidates that I would support.
g I've been given some new responsibilities which I think will be interesting, but I'll need to manage a new team, and they're located all over the world. I don't have much international experience and I'm worried about whether I can really do this.
h We've got so much going on at the moment – we're in the middle of the ISO90001 audit and we've just introduced a new IT system. I just don't think this is the time to introduce a change programme as well.

Let's talk

8 Think of a problem you have or have had regarding a change process (for example, difficulty in motivating a member of your team or having to tell staff about redundancy). With a partner, set up a coaching discussion. Use the structure below to help you move from identifying the problem to finding a solution.

Stage 1: Identify the issue (What is the problem you are trying to solve? Of all of the issues, which is the priority?)
Stage 2: Explore possibilities (What have you already tried? What might work best?)
Stage 3: Agree steps (What do you need to do to reach your goal?)
Stage 4: Overcome barriers (What is stopping you? What resources do you need?)
Stage 5: Conclude (Summarise the action plan. How are you going to measure your progress?)

4 Overcoming resistance

C Professional skills: Dealing with the consequences of redundancies

Think about it

1 Think about a change experience you have been through. How did you feel when you first heard about the change, and how did your feelings alter over time? Do you remember how others reacted?

2 Have you had experience of offering people voluntary redundancy or telling people they have lost their job? How did you communicate it? How did the person react?

Read this

3 Read this article, then answer the questions on page 43.

Downsizing: Leading those that remain
by Robert Bacal

Downsizing, right-sizing, lay-offs or workforce adjustment – whatever the current 'correct' terminology, the fact remains that it is the most difficult thing that managers will deal with in their careers. There are two issues regarding downsizing. First, the period of downsizing brings with it incredible anxiety for everyone. While this is the period of greatest short-term stress, it is an acute situation. The second problem, and one of much more long-term significance, is the issue of those that remain. Somehow managers have to deal with the fall-out from the downsizing process, and move their organisations beyond the grief, the anger and the loss of morale that characterises these major organisational events. It is those that remain that will determine what happens to the organisation. We are going to talk about the long-term issues here.

In the first few weeks after downsizing, even those who still have jobs will feel a lot of difficult things. Grief, anger, a sense of betrayal and depression are common 'normal' reactions. Typically, productivity drops as people work through their feelings by talking with each other. This also applies to you as the leader of your organisation. However, as a leader, you have an important role to play in helping employees get past the initial reactions. During this time, it is important that you do not pressurise employees unduly, either in the areas of increasing productivity or in expressing feelings about the change. Some people want to talk, others do not. Some will work harder, some will not. Your job is to help by gently talking to them, both in group settings and individually, about their reactions and how you can help. Listening is key here. Ask questions and keep your own comments to a minimum, and don't pressurise people. By showing concern and interest, you will be working towards repairing the sense of broken trust that accompanies downsizing.

During this period, you need to take stock of your own emotional situation. Your ability to lead people through the tough times will depend on your own physical and emotional health. Try not to cut yourself off. Talking to colleagues outside your organisation is a good idea, or at least expressing your own feelings to someone unconnected with your organisation. If you find yourself affected by sleeplessness, mood swings, depression and guilt, don't hesitate to take advantage of support services that are available.

The initial shock of downsizing is likely to linger for some time. Unfortunately, you and your staff have goals to accomplish, people to serve. At some point, there is a need to get on with it, to normalise the situation. The situation in your organisation can be helped if you start to address any operational problems that might have been caused by the downsizing. Any shifting in staff will result in new challenges in terms of doing business, and there can be some confusion and chaos regarding how you are going to go about doing 'business' with fewer people. It is important to reduce the chaos. Normally, this will mean clarifying with staff any concerns they have about getting the business done, and problem-solving the issues. The longer that there is confusion, the more likely there will be permanent effects on organisational health and morale.

During this period, both group problem-solving meetings and individual discussions are appropriate and recommended. Bring *all* staff into the discussion, and make sure everyone is clear what they should be doing. While the feelings of employees are important during this phase, staff need to be slowly moved back to getting the job done. By getting clear understanding of the changes, you will create a climate of stability, which is necessary for the 'recovery' of people in the organisation.

adapted from http://work911.com

a What does Robert Bacal say is the lasting problem that managers face when reducing the number of employees in an organisation?
b Which two things can managers do to help employees through the 'emotional' stage following downsizing?
c What does Bacal suggest that leaders should do for themselves during these difficult times?
d What operational problems can occur as a result of reducing staff numbers?
e How can you help people 'recover' following the kind of change described?

Focus on language

challenged
concerned
curious
excited
insecure
interested
motivated
pleased
unhappy
worried

4 a Use one or more of the adjectives from the box on the left to describe how you might feel when:
   a a new process or system is introduced.
   b you have to travel much more.
   c you gain more responsibility.
   d your company is bought by an organisation with a different culture.
   e you have to learn a new language.
   f you have to start working virtually (i.e. not meeting your colleagues face to face).

b Can you add any more adjectives to the list?

5 Complete the advice below for dealing with the consequences of downsizing using the verbs from the box.

| address | ask | bring | clarify | create | hesitate | make sure |
| pressurise | problem-solve | take | take stock | show | work |

a Don't .... employees unduly, either in the areas of increasing productivity or in expressing feelings about the change.
b .... questions and keep your own comments to a minimum.
c .... concern and interest.
d .... towards repairing the sense of broken trust that accompanies downsizing.
e .... of your own emotional situation.
f Don't .... to .... advantage of support services that are available.
g .... any operational problems that might have been caused by the downsizing.
h .... with staff any concerns they have about getting the business done.
i .... the issues.
j .... all staff into the discussion.
k .... everyone is clear what they should be doing.
l .... a climate of stability.

Let's talk

6 Following a change, roles often become confused, and people can feel insecure as a result. Clarifying roles and responsibilities is essential. With a partner, practise asking and answering these questions.
- What is your role?
- Who do you communicate with, and how?
- What information do you need, and what information do you produce? Who else needs it?
- Whose work do you monitor, and who monitors your work?
- What do you decide, and who with?
- What budget responsibility do you have, if any?
- What are your targets and milestones? How does this contribute to the overall goal? Who is responsible for the overall goal?

(adapted from MIM Comfort/Franklin p.87)

D Intercultural competence: Understanding motivation across cultures

1 Look at these factors that can motivate people. What are the most important motivational factors at work for you? As a group, find out which are the most common answers.

- a good work–life balance
- teamwork
- harmony at work
- financial reward
- job status
- consensus decision-making
- clear objectives
- supporting others
- bonus-linked targets
- social events
- recognition of achievement

2 Change can increase motivation for some and decrease motivation for others. What is your experience?

3 How could you find out what motivates the people you work with? How would you do this in an international context?

4 Some companies place more emphasis on getting the work done and on productivity (task-oriented), while others may focus on maintaining good relationships and keeping morale high (relationship-oriented). If that company culture changed, how would that affect your motivation?

5 Look at this list of management actions and complete the table below, according to whether you think each one relates more to a task-oriented company or style, or a relationship-oriented company or style.

supporting work–life balance   fostering teamwork
recognising individual achievement   setting financial goals
encouraging consensus decision-making   MBO (managing by objectives)
giving reward for supporting others   setting bonus-linked targets
arranging social or team-building events   focusing on returns for shareholders

task-oriented	relationship-oriented
	supporting work–life balance

6 In your work situation, what could you do to help people through change and to increase their motivation? Choose one of the items from the list in Exercise 5 and, with a partner, decide how you could implement this.

7 One way to find out what motivates people is to ask them some simple questions. Ask one or two of your partners these questions and find out what motivates them.
- What kind of work environment makes you productive?
- How do you define success?
- How do you like to be managed?
- What makes you unhappy about your working life?
- What would you change in your current working life if you could?

Case study: Overcoming resistance

Background Pilbara Mining, a large Australian mining organisation, has ambitions to expand by investing in mining in Africa. It is doing this by buying up smaller companies. It has recently acquired Declaire Engineering, a South African company that specialises in mining equipment and engineering. Declaire Engineering has been struggling financially, which is why it has accepted Pilbara Mining's offer. However, Declaire Engineering's management is still well connected to local politicians. Through these relationships, Pilbara Mining hopes to gain access to new business in the region.

The people at Declaire Engineering are still unsure of what the acquisition will mean for them. In the short term, the key objective is for the team to find budget savings of 20% in year one, in order to create a more efficient organisation.

Situation Ben is a leader from Pilbara Mining who is working with a team, managing facilities and allowances. The team includes staff from both companies. Key to its success is overcoming resistance and helping people to adapt. Although Ben has to get results from his team, he must also maintain motivation. Things are not going very well, and some of the people from Declaire Engineering are not engaging with the objectives he has set.

🎧 **18** Listen to part of a meeting with Ben and two of his team members, Guillaume and Ellen, to find out why they are resisting the changes.

a What does Guillaume feel is wrong with the team?
b Whose responsibility does Guillaume think it is to improve team relations?
c What expectation does Ben have about the team and its goals?
d Why isn't Ellen sure about the target and how to achieve it?
e What problem does Guillaume see with the reward system that Ben is suggesting?
f What do Guillaume and Ellen prioritise, the task or the relationships? What about Ben?

Tasks 1 You have been brought in as a consultant to support Ben. What do you think are some of the key motivational factors for the Declaire Engineering employees that you heard? Look at this list and tick the factors that you think are most important to the employees.

a autonomy ☐
b good relationships ☐
c team recognition ☐
d individual reward ☐
e support from management ☐
f financial reward ☐

2 **In the meeting, Ben said:**

I think you all have to realise that things can't be relaxed and friendly all the time. Declaire Engineering was inefficient – that's why it's been taken over. I think the reward system will encourage people to be more ambitious, so it'll help to change the company culture for the better.

Do you think Ben's assumption about the objective of the reward system is right in this context? Do you think this will increase motivation?

3 **Form small groups and look at some of the obstacles to change that Ben faces. How could he deal with these? Which do you think would be the easiest to deal with, and which the most difficult?**
- Unfamiliar leadership style
- Not knowing the team members well
- People not used to taking responsibility for targets
- Lack of clarity about roles/responsibilities/tasks
- Mismatch of values (e.g. target-oriented vs relationship-orientated cultures)

4 **Present to the group some actions that will help Ben maintain the motivation of his team and deal with all or some of the obstacles.**

E Language reference

Read through the key words and phrases below. Add any other useful words and expressions which you feel are important for you to learn. Make sure you find the time to review these words and phrases regularly and to use them at work.

Carrying out individual interviews
How do you feel about …?
I understand that you are (not) …
Am I right in thinking that you are …?
How can I help you …? / What can I do to help you …?

Coaching/Supporting people through change
Identify the issue
Can you prioritise what you see as the main problem? / Shall we focus on that today?
Explore possibilities
What have you done to establish your role and responsibilities?
How could you clarify what you and others should be doing?
What have you already tried?
What exactly is stopping you from doing your job well?
What do you need to do to reach your goal?
What resources do you need?
Agree steps
Could you just go through what we've talked about?
What are you going to do, and by when?
Overcome barriers
What could stop you from achieving your goals?
Conclude
How will you know if you've been successful?
How are you going to measure your progress?

Problem-solving / Moving people on
Show empathy
I understand you're anxious about the changes we're implementing.
You seem to be worried about the way things have changed.
I'd like you to know that I do understand your position.

State purpose
The reason I'm calling you today is to …
I'd like to invite you to a meeting to discuss these issues.

Recognise value
That sounds like a really good idea.

Intervene in a conversation
Could I just interrupt you?

Clarify a point
I think it's important to clarify …
If I can recap, you said that …

Reassure
What can I do to help you move on?

Writing task Look again at the Case study on page 45. Ben, the team leader, has set up a blog where team members can contribute with updates and success stories. Imagine you are Deena, a team member; you are going to write the first contribution on the recent successful team-building activity. Include these points:
- three-day event (two days working on leadership and decision-making, one day focusing on building a raft and navigating some rapids on the Orange River as a team)
- Ben was impressed by the co-operation of the team.
- The team appreciated Ben's focus on goals, which meant that the raft was built on time.
- Ben fell into the river and was thankful that the team members rescued him.
- Ellen showed leadership by getting the team to stop the raft crashing into some rocks.
- They had learned that:
  – it was important to work together to ensure that creative ideas emerged, but also to focus on goals to make sure the target was realised
  – in times of crisis, it was important to support others and to make decisions quickly.

F Change-management working tips and personal action plan

1 Take a few minutes to reflect on these tips on managing change which arise from this unit. How far do you agree with each one? Which do you think is the most important, and which ideas are the most useful?

> **TIP 1**
> People need time to work through the emotions of change. It's important for leaders to have individual interviews and meetings with team members in order to listen to grievances.
> Ideas for dealing with problems:
> - Identify who might lose from the change process and what they will lose. Focus on possible gains that might come from the change and try to 'sell these' to the individuals concerned.
> - Identify the influencers in the organisation, those with a wide network of contacts or those who have the support of other people. Listen to and negotiate with these people to get their support for the change.

> **TIP 2**
> It's important that each employee finds their own way of dealing with the change and that they take responsibility for finding solutions to problems. Coaching and mentoring skills can be important for leaders to develop in order to help people do this.
> Ideas for different ways of helping people cope with change:
> - Dedicate time and energy to listening, clarifying, supporting people and problem-solving.
> - Move people back as quickly as possible to getting the job done. Repeat what the targets of the change are and give people responsibility, recognition and reward for working towards and achieving targets.

> **TIP 3**
> When you are working in a complex international environment, it's important that all the key people involved support the change and are motivated to achieve targets, as it's impossible for leaders to push through change alone.
> Ideas for motiving people through change:
> - Identify what obstacles might stop people from accepting change and what might motivate people to support it; these could be quite different from one country/context to another.
> - Ask questions, observe and work with people to remove obstacles by making changes that increase their motivation.
> - Build the team, open and strengthen communication channels and build trust through face-to-face team-building events or retreats.

Personal action plan 2 Take 15 minutes to review the unit. Write down at least three important points that you have learned and that you want to apply to your change-management practice. Then commit to a schedule to implement your learning and think about how you can check if you have been successful.

	what I have learned and want to apply in my change-management practice	when/how I will apply this in my change-management practice	how I will check if I have applied it
1			
2			
3			

5 Influencing people

AIMS
A To build rapport through networking
B To use influencing skills
C To influence people through storytelling
D To influence people across cultures

A Discussion and listening

Think about it

> Networking is simply the cultivating of mutually beneficial, give-and-take, win–win relationships. It works best, however, when emphasising the 'give' part.
>
> Bob Burg (1958–), author and speaker

1 **Discuss these questions with a partner.**
   a What kinds of network exist in your organisation (e.g. formally structured teams, groups who socialise informally, company football team)?
   b What kinds of network do you belong to, and how did you become a part of them?
   c How can you create better formal or informal networks in your organisation?

Listen to this

2 a 🎧 **19** Listen to Farida Feuillet, a senior manager in a large energy company, talking about how she uses networks in her organisation to spread change. According to Farida, which kinds of people in organisations can really influence others to change?

   b Give an example of a formal and an informal network, as identified by Farida in her organisation.

3 🎧 **20** Listen to the second part of the interview and answer these questions.
   a What three things does Farida mention that describe how people 'build rapport'?
   b According to Farida, what other two skills are needed to be a good influencer?

4 🎧 **21** Listen to Thomas Johansen, who has been identified by Farida Feuillet as a potential influencer within the company. His role is in technical support for international sales and he has a lot of contact with global subsidiaries. Complete these comments Thomas makes about what he does to build rapport and encourage networking in his company.

I travel a lot, as I like to meet people face to face, and we **(a)** .... through our personal Facebook accounts. I also **(b)** .... people .... other useful contacts – this helps the team work better, especially when we're all over the world.

I try to increase my visibility and improve connections between people. I do this by arranging social activities and sports teams at my factory and I **(c)** .... an annual international meeting. This is a great opportunity to **(d)** .... different groups ....

I'm told that I **(e)** .... the global teams because I try to see their position, by listening to them and asking questions. Then I make management aware of their situation. I also **(f)** .... communication in virtual meetings between HQ and the subsidiaries, especially if some people don't speak English so well.

Because I **(g)** .... positive relationships and encourage **(h)** .... in the company, senior managers often ask me to help **(i)** .... people to accept change.

Focus on language **5** Complete this table with the correct forms of the words.

verb	noun	adjective	example
connect	(a)	(b)	We have a (c) .... through an old workmate.
(d)	network networker	(e)	I think most people don't know how to (f) .... properly.
persuade	(g)	(h)	She can be really (i) .... I was completely convinced.
facilitate	(j)	(k)	We couldn't have done it without Sue's (l) .... skills. She got everyone on board.
(m)	(n)	inclusive	Don't forget to (o) .... all the team members in that invitation!
(p)	supporter	(q)	My colleague always listens to my views. He is so (r) ....
organise	(s)	(t)	People tell me that I'm a good (u) .... , so I arrange most events.

6 Complete these phrases with a suitable word from Exercise 5. In most cases, there is more than one possible answer.
  a join a ....
  b .... a meeting / conference call
  c .... skills
  d a good/bad/(in)efficient ....
  e a(n) .... colleague/boss

Let's talk **7** Are you good at building networks and rapport? Ask a partner these questions and note down their answers.
  a How do you build relationships with people you don't know? What rapport-building strategies have you tried? (e.g. contacting people through LinkedIn, introducing yourself at an event, inviting someone for lunch, offering to help someone, etc.)
  b How do you meet people you know? (e.g. social meetings, lunch, Facebook)
  c How do you bring together people who don't know each other? (e.g. organise events, meetings, etc.)
  d How do you support the work of others? (e.g. provide information, put them in touch with a useful contact, help them deal with problems, etc.)
  e When did you last to try to understand another person's point of view? What did you do to show this?

8 Choose a 'rapport-building' strategy. Go around the rest of the class and try to find out three new things about two colleagues.

B Communication skills: Using influencing skills

Think about it 1 Describe what happened the last time you had to negotiate an agreement or convince someone to do something.

2 Do you know or use a special technique for negotiating or convincing people? Tell the group about it.

Listen to this 3 🎧 **22** Listen to a discussion between Al, a supply-chain manager at an automotive parts company, and Consuela, the production manager at one of the company's plants in Spain. Answer these questions.
   a How does Al begin the meeting with Consuela?
   b How has Al helped Consuela in the past?

4 🎧 **23** Listen to the next part of their discussion and answer these questions.
   a What is Al's objective?
   b What is Consuela's main problem?
   c Do you think Al is listening to Consuela? Give examples.
   d What is Consuela's priority?
   e How does Al address Consuela's priority?

5 🎧 **24** Listen to the final part of the discussion and answer these questions.
   a What common ground exists between Al and Consuela?
   b What solution does Al find with Consuela?
   c Does Al achieve his objective?

6 a Match each of the negotiating words from the box with a definition below (a–i).

| bargaining benefits compromise concession consensus |
| disadvantage disagreement leverage priorities proposal |

   a When parties don't have the same opinion
   b The process of proposing and counter-proposing
   c When all parties have the same opinion
   d When one party has less power or influence than the other
   e When a position is put forward
   f The power to influence a person or situation
   g The positive points
   h The action of giving something up in order to move forward (*two words*)
   i The most important points

b Now complete each of these phrases with an appropriate word from above. In some cases, more than one is possible.
   a make a ...
   b reach a ...
   c be at a ...
   d put forward a ...
   e have some ...
   f have a ...
   g to engage in collective ...

Focus on language **7** Look at the model below for influencing, in which Al breaks down communication into three parts. Match each of these phrases (a–m) to one of the parts (1–3).

a Can I ask you what your priorities are over the next couple of years?
b Can we agree, then, that the sooner we implement the new system, the better it is for both of us?
c How are things going for you?
d I don't know ... I guess we could do that.
e I hear what you're saying ... Have you considered the benefits you'll get?
f I'd like to hear your views and find out how you feel about this.
g It's good of you to come over today.
h Nice to meet you face to face at last! Would you like a coffee?
i So, can I summarise the key points?
j So we have an agreement. Can you draw up a schedule?
k To save more costs, I can second one of my people to your team for, say, six months. How does that sound?
l We're working towards the same goal here, so let's see what we can do with the budget.
m What extra costs exactly will you incur?

Tips for influencing

1 Rapport/relationship-building
- Get on the same wavelength.
- Create a harmonious, positive atmosphere.
- Build rapport.

2 Active listening
- Understand the other person's point of view.
- Focus on their needs.
- Take time to listen to them carefully and find out about their interests and expectations.
- Clarify their arguments and assess the logic of their reasoning.

3 Persuading/convincing
- **Balancing argument**
  - Outline the benefits of the proposal and argue your case with logic.
  - List the issues which are important to both sides and identify the key issues and any areas of common ground.
- **Conceding**
  - Know when to compromise.
  - Offer concessions where necessary.
- **Moving to agreement**
  - Decide on a course of action and come to an agreement.

Let's talk **8** Work with a partner.

Student A: Turn to page 89.
Student B: Turn to page 92.

Choose one of the scenarios and, using some of the language from Exercise 7, persuade a colleague to change the way they do something.

C Professional skills: Influencing people through storytelling

Think about it

> *People don't really buy a product, service or idea; they buy the story that's attached to it.*
>
> Michael Margolis, CEO of Get Storied

1 Look at the quote above. What does Michael Margolis mean by 'the story' that's attached to a product, service or idea? In what ways do companies 'create stories' around a brand?

2 Telling stories to influence people is used internationally. What brands do you buy, and what stories do marketers attach to them?

Read this 3 A flip-flop is a type of shoe. Read the story of the flip-flops known as 'Havaianas', then answer the questions on page 53.

Brazil's rubber soul

Introduction
Today, the Havaiana flip-flop is one of the best-known fashion brands to come out of Brazil. One of the directors of the parent company that produces Havaianas tells us that in 2011, 210 million pairs of Havaianas were sold worldwide. Even with 15 per cent of total production exported to some 80 countries, enough of the sandals were sold in 2011 for nearly every man, woman and child in Brazil. They are famous for their exotic colours, flashy designs and universal appeal, just as stylish on the beach as at a party or about town. The marketing director commented that customers have a very strong, emotional connection to Havaianas and that they are loyal to the brand. She said that the image Havaianas portray is of simple pleasures, happiness and freedom.

History
However, the Havaianas flip-flops had not always been a success. In 1993, the parent company was struggling, and it had almost given up on the brand, fearing that they were a flop. Havaianas were sold at a low cost in cheap supermarkets. There were only four colours, and the advertising slogan said 'They don't smell, and the strap doesn't tear'. The humble Havaianas were positioned by cleaning products so maids could find them and by building materials for construction workers. As a result, the customer base came from the lowest class in Brazilian society. Havaianas became such a basic for the poor in Brazil that they were included on the list of basic necessities, such as rice and beans, that the government used to calculate cost-of-living increases. Havaianas were synonymous with poverty.

Problem
From 1988, sales started to decline, and by the early 1990s, domestic competitors were beginning to eat away at Havaianas' market share. When the company looked at the customer base, they found that wealthier customers were buying flip-flops, but they would only wear them inside, as they were too ashamed to wear them out. The brand executives realised they had to upgrade the image, so they shifted strategy by 180 degrees and managed an extremely difficult brand re-positioning. In 1994, Havaianas started to introduce new lines and shades of sandals; they were packaged in boxes and given better positioning in stores; and sophisticated actors were brought in for advertising campaigns.

Resolution
By the end of the 1990s, middle- and upper-class Brazilians, who wouldn't have been seen dead in Havaianas before, were buying up multiple shades and designs for all occasions. Havaianas have come a long way and have transcended both their modest origins and the country's borders to become an object of desire the world over. The brand has successfully associated itself with positive Latin American characteristics such as sensuality, youth and joy. Once an embarrassment only worn by the domestic help, these days they are sold at Bloomingdale's and Neiman Marcus and coveted by Hollywood actors such as Brad Pitt and Angelina Jolie, European royals and suburban ladies from Seattle to Seoul. The plan, aimed at rebranding Havaianas as a fashion accessory and associated brand building, has proved so successful that it has since become a business-school case study in marketing.

a How did the parent company change the story of the Havaianas brand?
b What do Havaianas symbolise today, according to the marketing director?
c How did the positioning of Havaianas flip-flops originally target the least wealthy people in Brazilian society?
d Why did people from higher social classes only use Havaianas flip-flops inside the house in the past?
e In the article, the marketing director says that people 'have a very strong emotional connection to Havaianas'. What do you understand by this?
f Identify three pieces of evidence from the article that show that a brand transformation has been achieved in relation to Havaianas flip-flops.

Focus on language 4 Find marketing terms in the article that go with these sets of words.
a .... repositioning / building / value / transformation / awareness / loyalty / strategy
b .... campaign / executive / agency / department / budget / slogan
c improve / upgrade / damage / create / change your ....

5 Complete these sentences about Havaianas flip-flops using an appropriate word from Exercise 4 in the correct form.
a The makers of Havaianas successfully *repositioned* the brand in the 1990s.
b The Havaianas .... slogan read 'They don't smell, and the strap doesn't tear'.
c Their image was .... partly by moving the products to better locations in stores and putting them in boxes.
d Slapstick comedians were replaced by sophisticated actors in advertising ....
e The Havaianas flip-flops went through a brand .... to convince the rich and famous to wear them.
f Brand .... will be key to their continuing success.
g The Havaianas story is an example of how the .... of a product can be changed radically through marketing.

6 Retell the Havaianas story. Make some notes under these headings and use some of the phrases given to help you.
- Introduction (set the scene)
  Today, ...
- History (connect with the past, give the background)
  However, it wasn't always like that ...
  In the beginning, ...
  In 1994, ...
- Problem (create suspense / what needed to change?)
  After ... Then ... One day ... From 1988, ...
- Resolution (and looking to the future)
  By the end of the '90s, ...
  It turned out ...
  In the end ...
  In fact, ...
  Since ...
  The next step will be ...

Let's talk 7 Tell a transformation story about yourself, your company or a product or service you know. Try to make it personal and create an emotional connection with your audience.

5 Influencing people

D Intercultural competence: Influencing people across cultures

1 What competences or skills can you develop to improve your ability to influence internationally? Discuss with the group which training courses people have done or seen to help develop influencing skills.

2 Read these three 'influencing' competences from Worldwork's *The International Profiler*, then match each of the comments below (a–f) to one of the comptences (1–3).

1 Rapport
Exhibits warmth and attentiveness when building relationships in a variety of contexts. Puts a premium on choosing verbal and non-verbal behaviours that are comfortable for international counterparts, thus building a sense of 'we'. Able in the longer-term to meet the criteria for trust required by international partners.

2 Range of styles
Has a variety of means for influencing people across a range of international contexts. This gives greater capacity to 'lead' an international partner in a style with which they feel comfortable.

3 Sensitivity to context
Recognises where political power lies in organisations and understands how best to use this to achieve objectives. Puts energy into absorbing the different cultural contexts in which messages are sent and decisions are made.

a 'I know that John plays golf with the CEO, and although John's not that senior, the CEO passes on what's going on lower down in the organisation, so if we can get our message through to John, it might help our proposal.'
b 'Why don't we arrange a night out and invite the guys from the subsidiaries? It'd be a good opportunity to get to know them better.'
c 'Those Americans don't have much time for our long-winded discussions in meetings … maybe if we want to get them on our side, we should try and keep it short?'
d 'I've noticed that our clients always want to refer to the owner of the company before making any decisions. Do you think we should try to find a way to get to know him?'
e 'Rather than getting straight down to business, shall we have a coffee first?'
f 'You could try listening more, trying to understand their position, rather than telling them how they should work all the time.'

3 🎧 **25** Eric Huang is an intercultural coach. Listen to him talking about how to develop skills for influencing people internationally, then answer these questions.
a What examples does Eric give of how you can develop relationship-building skills?
b What does he say is the foundation of relationships?
c How does he suggest adapting communication styles with Scandinavian, Latin American and Asian cultures?
d What kinds of people does he think you may need to influence first?

4 Think about how good you are at the three influencing skills discussed by Eric Huang. Ask a partner these questions and make a note of their responses.

1 Building rapport and relationships
a How important is it to have a good relationship with someone in order to work together successfully?
b Is it common to socialise outside work?
c What is your strategy for getting to know someone?

2 Adapting your communication style to suit your partners
d Have you ever found you were too direct/indirect?
e When do you tell and when do you ask, in order to achieve results?
f In what different ways do you communicate with your boss/colleagues/clients?

3 Being political
g Which different kinds of people do you have to influence to achieve your goals?
h Which 'persuasion' strategies have worked for you in the past?
i How is the term *influencing* perceived?

5 Which of the three skills would you like to develop further?

Case study: Influencing a new team in Brazil

Background

Christina Soberg is a manager in the quality department of a large cellulose company. She is Swedish and 30 years old. The company has recently entered a joint venture with a South American partner. She has been sent to Brazil for a year to tell the managers how they should implement the quality system used in Europe. This is necessary, as the cellulose products will now be exported to Europe and they must have the necessary certification. She doesn't know any of the people in the Brazilian organisation and she doesn't speak Portuguese, but she is an expert in the quality system that must be implemented.

Situation

Christina has been in Brazil for three months. Her original goal was to have the quality system in place and to be at the next stage of implementing the certification process. However, she has experienced some resistance and delays, and the project is already two weeks behind schedule. She is getting increasingly frustrated with the local quality team and has called her manager, Harri, who is now based in Sweden but has worked in Brazil in the past. She has told him that the local Quality Manager, Marcio, really wants to take over the whole project, as he keeps interfering; Claudia, the Quality Certification Senior Technician, seems more interested in having fun than working; and Rodrigo, the Quality Control Engineer and team leader, appears moody and obviously doesn't like her.

Harri has organised a conference call with Marcio, Claudia and Rodrigo to find out what's going on. Listen to three excerpts from the conference call and match Harri's advice to Christina (a–d) to each problem being raised by the team members (1–3).

🎧 26 1 Marcio (Quality Manager)

🎧 27 2 Claudia (Quality Certification Senior Technician)

🎧 28 3 Rodrigo (Quality Control Engineer / team leader)

a Brazilian communication is typically quite indirect, and you may have offended this person, so you should adapt your style.
b Seniority and experience are respected, and senior people tend to be well connected. You need to gain the support of this person to help influence the rest of the team.
c The local team has other priorities in the region which are important to understand in order to manage the overall workload. Find out what other goals are important for this team member.
d Relationships and social contact are important. If you spend some time getting to know this person, you could engage them more in the process.

Tasks

1 With a partner, imagine you are in Christina's position. Having listened to Harri's advice, what are you going to do to influence the team members and the team as a whole, in order to get the project back on track? When you have agreed some steps, note them on a flip chart.

2 Work with a partner.
   Student A: See below.
   Student B: Turn to page 93.

> **Student A**
> You are Christina. Listen to the team members and their points of view and suggestions. Use some of the actions gathered by the group to help you influence them. Your objective is to get them to support you and to prioritise the implementation of the new quality system and certification project.

5 Influencing people

E Language reference

Read through the key words and phrases below. Add any other useful words and expressions which you feel are important for you to learn. Make sure you find the time to review these words and phrases regularly and to use them at work.

Characteristics of good influencers/networkers

connect people
make things happen
build rapport
make an effort to get to know new people
listen and take an interest in others
try to see the world through the eyes of others

meet people face to face
make useful contacts
increase visibility
arrange social activities
build positive relationships
support people
encourage/facilitate

Language for negotiating/persuading

Creating a positive atmosphere
Nice to meet you face to face at last – would you like a coffee?
It's good of you to come over today.
I appreciate you giving your time.
It's really great to meet you in person.

Showing you're listening
I'd like to hear your views and find out how you feel about this.
Can I ask you what your priorities are?
What would you like to happen?
What is your position?

Clarifying arguments / Finding agreement
I hear what you're saying ...
Have you considered the benefits of ...?
When you say ... , can you tell me exactly ...?
We're working towards the same goal here, so let's see what we can do with ...
So, can I summarise the key points?
Can we agree, then, that this is good for both of us?
How does that sound?
So, we have an agreement.
Can you draw up a schedule/contract/proposal?

Marketing verb phrases

reposition/transform a brand
have/develop brand loyalty / a brand strategy
increase brand awareness / brand loyalty
launch an advertising campaign
engage an advertising executive/agency
work for an advertising department
increase / decrease / stick to an advertising budget
create an advertising slogan
improve/upgrade/damage/create/change your image

Storytelling language

Today ...
However, it wasn't always like that. In the beginning ...
In 1993, ... / From 1988, ...
After ... Then ... One day ...
By the end of the '90s, ...
It turned out ...
In the end, ...
In fact, ...
Since ...
The next step will be ...

Writing task Write your own change story. Focus on the message you want to sell (about yourself, an idea or a product). Use the storytelling structure from Section C Exercise 6 and some of the language from this section to help you.

F Change-management working tips and personal action plan

1 Take a few minutes to reflect on these tips on managing change which arise from this unit. How far do you agree with each one? Which do you think is the most important, and which ideas are the most useful?

TIP 1

Build relationships with those you wish to influence. Remember to think about the people who influence the influencers – you may need to convince the majority that your idea is a good one before the people at the top will accept it.
Ideas for building positive relationships:
- Find out what is important to your partners and take an interest in these things.
- Increase your visibility through the company and represent your team strongly. Encourage the development of networks by bringing people together.
- Choose behaviours that are comfortable for your international counterparts.
- Learn to recognise where political power lies in organisations and understand how best to use this to achieve objectives.

TIP 2

Developing negotiating skills is essential when implementing change.
Ideas for developing negotiating skills:
- Clarify the arguments of the other party and assess the logic of their reasoning.
- Outline the benefits of the proposal and argue your case with logic.
- List the issues which are important to both sides and identify areas of common ground.
- Know when to compromise. Offer concessions where necessary.
- Decide on a course of action and come to an agreement.

TIP 3

Storytelling is central to human existence, common to every culture. Stories are recognisable patterns in which we find meaning and make sense of the world. Using anecdotes and storytelling can be a very powerful way to get a change message across.
Ideas for incorporating storytelling:
- Listen to one of your favourite business leaders or speakers telling inspirational stories on YouTube; note down the expressions they use and how they make an emotional connection. Incorporate these words and techniques into your own communication.
- Use the storytelling structure to tell your stories: set the scene, give the history, describe a problem or crisis and come to a resolution.

Personal action plan 2 Take 15 minutes to review the unit. Write down at least three important points that you have learned and that you want to apply to your change-management practice. Then commit to a schedule to implement your learning and think about how you can check if you have been successful.

	what I have learned and want to apply in my change-management practice	when/how I will apply this in my change-management practice	how I will check if I have applied it
1			
2			
3			

6 Developing change leaders

AIMS
A To identify the skills that change leaders need
B To give and receive feedback
C To train for change
D To develop change leaders across cultures

A Discussion and listening

Think about it

> Leadership creates the systems that managers manage and changes them in fundamental ways to take advantage of opportunities and to avoid hazards.
>
> John Kotter (1947–), leadership and change expert

1 Discuss with a partner how you would define a 'change leader'.

2 Describe an effective change leader that you have known. What made them effective?

Listen to this

3 🎧 29 Ana Pedrosa is an HR director at a global pharmaceutical firm, based in Switzerland. She is asked about the key skills that managers need to manage change in their organisations. Listen and answer these questions.
   a What does Ana feel is the most important thing a manager needs to be able to do to successfully manage change?
   b How did Ana develop the ability to adapt her messages and style of presentation?
   c What other benefit did Ana get from her interpersonal and intercultural training?

4 🎧 30 Listen to François Bertrand, the Operations Director of a French luxury-goods company, and answer these questions.
   a According to François, what skill can help managers when having difficult conversations?
   b What skill is important to develop in order to manage the people who remain after a reorganisation?
   c What two skills does François say he developed to learn how to motivate people?
   d What does François consider to be two important skills, but ones you can't be trained to exercise?

5 Which of the skills mentioned by Ana and François do you think are the most important to develop?

6 Which other skills do you consider to be useful for a change leader to learn?

Focus on language

7 Look at these nine leadership actions which are extremely important when implementing change. Which would you most benefit from developing, to support the challenges you face?

1 clarifying roles	2 improving team understanding	3 giving feedback
4 providing direction	5 supporting people	6 encouraging co-operation
7 organising people	8 resolving conflict	9 representing teams

58   6 Developing change leaders

8 Match one of the leadership actions from Exercise 7 (1–9) to each of these descriptions (a–i).

Example: a 2

a Who are we? Get to know team members and key players by building relationships.
b Where are we going? Communicate common goals and benefits clearly to gain commitment.
c How do we plan to do it? Co-ordinate resources (time, people, money) and generate guidelines for working in the team.
d Who does what? Ensure people are clear about their responsibilities and those of others.
e What help is needed? Consider the benefits of mentoring, coaching, facilitating and networking.
f How are we performing? Motivate people and improve performance through constructive comments on individual and team efforts.
g How are we seen in the organisation? Promote the work of the team across the company. Present and 'sell' a team's project effectively.
h Where are the problems between people generated? Manage internal and external resistance.
i How are we working together as a team? Enable people to work together effectively and move towards synergy.

9 Chameleon Training is a company that offers programmes in leading change and innovation. Complete the programme objectives below with the words and phrases from the box.

| comfort zone | compensate | creative | empower | feedback |
| innovate | judgement | multiple ideas | team-profiling | |

Leading change and innovation

In our training programme, you will:

a develop methods to look at problems in .... ways.
b use a .... tool to identify and understand the different working styles of your team members.
c build on your team's strengths, and recognise and .... for its weaknesses.
d practise generating .... and stretching your thinking outside your ....
e learn to look at possibilities and consider ideas without ....
f build the ability to give more positive and constructive ....
g .... the creativity of others and motivate them to ....

Let's talk 10 What training or development programmes have you taken part in? Which helped you most as a change leader?

11 Work in groups of three. Imagine that you are all leaders of the same company. You are planning a training programme for your best people to develop them as future change leaders. Decide on three objectives that you will prioritise, what type of training you will organise and how much time you will need. Then present your programme to the other groups.

B Communication skills: Giving and receiving feedback

Think about it 1 Have you ever given or been given feedback? What was your experience?

2 When giving feedback on performance, what do you think is important to consider?

Listen to this 3 🎧 **31** Bill Adams is a senior manager of a specialist steel manufacturer in England. Karin Schmidt is a manager who has recently been brought in from Germany to support the UK business. The company operates in a very competitive environment, and the price of steel has slumped recently. Karin has been responsible for implementing major organisational changes across the business to make it leaner and fitter. Listen to Bill reviewing Karin's performance during the change programme, then answer these questions.

   a What is Karin's view of the work she has done so far?
   b What has Bill noticed about the work Karin has done?
   c What negative outcome of the change effort does Karin mention?
   d What does Bill want Karin to do more of next time?

4 🎧 **32** Listen to the rest of the conversation between Bill and Karin and answer these questions.

   a Why does Karin suggest she may not always understand people?
   b What three things does Bill think would benefit Karin to help her with her work in future?

Focus on language 5 Feedback is a useful way of reviewing performance and agreeing to change behaviour in the future. Look at this five-step feedback process and match the examples of language from Tracks 31 and 32 below (a–j) with each step (1–5).

   1 Say what you have observed.   *a, …*
   2 Say what effect this behaviour has had.
   3 Show support, appreciation and encouragement.
   4 Ask what could be improved in future.
   5 Say what changes you want to see.

   a I've noticed that you've been working very hard …
   b We've seen some interesting new ideas coming from your people.
   c This means that people are starting to change the way they do things.
   d That's good to hear, thank you.
   e Can we talk about what needs to be improved?
   f Is there anything you think you could have done better?
   g I've noticed that you're very focused on the goals …
   h I'd like to see you focus more on the people, too.
   i What would you do differently next time?
   j How could I help you more?

| deal with |
| do |
| do |
| give |
| review |
| summarise |
| tell |
| think |
| try |

6 Complete these feedback expressions with verbs from the box on the left.

   a Could we .... the progress in the project so far?
   b Would you like to .... me some feedback on how I'm supporting you?
   c Could you .... me how you think things are going?
   d What do you think you could .... better?
   e How could you .... that problem?
   f Do you .... if you'd been more indirect, that team member wouldn't have been so offended?
   g What would you .... differently next time?
   h I think in future you could .... to adapt the way you communicate.
   i Could you .... the action points?

6 Developing change leaders

7 A sales director has noticed that one of the sales managers has omitted to upload his last report into the new CRM (customer relations management) system for the end of the month and needs to give him feedback on this. Rank these four statements (a–d) in order of directness (1 = most direct, 4 = least direct).

a Jag, I couldn't find your last SE Asia report on the system.

b Jag, you forgot to upload your last SE Asia report onto the system.

c *(To the whole team)* One important point to remember is to upload all sales reports onto the system by the end of each month. Could you all check that you've done this for your last sales report? Thank you.

d Jag, I'm afraid that the last SE Asia report seems to be missing on the system.

8 a Restate these direct phrases in a less direct manner.

a Juan, this report is useless.

b Mary, that presentation isn't going to persuade anyone, never mind the board.

c David, your e-mail was one of the rudest I've ever seen.

d Yvonne, the meetings you chair are a complete waste of time.

b Which level of directness do you most typically use? Which level of directness is most appropriate in your team?

Let's talk

9 Work in groups of three. Students A and B are going to discuss a work issue, while Student C observes the discussion and gives feedback afterwards.

Student A: See below.

Student B: Turn to page 93.

Student C: Turn to page 95.

If there is time, you can change roles and repeat the exercise.

Student A

You are Tom. You work for a food company which is internationalising. You are a sales director who has already worked in the UK, South America and Europe. Six months ago, you were moved to the HQ in Germany to lead the internationalisation team there and to develop a team of high potentials for future expatriate positions. These people will then go out to other locations to spread new ideas and methods and to develop their own teams. The first goal that you have set your team members is to be more open to the views of others and to resist judging ideas, in order to find more creative solutions to problems and to capitalise on diversity. You have been observing one of your team members, Ralf, during a meeting about how to integrate IT systems globally. Give Ralf some feedback. You noticed the following:

- He was leading the meeting in a very structured way, he kept the team focused on the agenda and he pushed the meeting along.
- He asked all the team members to contribute.
- He kept interrupting when a Spanish member of the team, Ramona, was trying to explain her idea.
- He was very quick to tell Ramona that her idea wouldn't work for the Eastern European part of their business.

You feel that next time, Ralf should build some 'brainstorming' time into the agenda for this type of meeting, he should listen and ask questions before interrupting, and he should recognise the value of Ramona's contribution and make sure it is explored fully with the whole group. He should reserve judgement.

C Professional skills: Training for change

Think about it 1 Discuss these questions with a partner.
  a What are the most common kinds of training in your organisation? How are training needs established?
  b Have you had any training or development in relation to managing change?

Read this 2 Read this article about the 'Toyota way', then decide whether the statements on page 63 are true (T) or false (F).

The 'Toyota way': translated for a new generation of managers

It is not uncommon to see coloured bar charts on the walls of American companies. These are usually showing the progress the company is making towards its goals. However, at Toyota's North American manufacturing plant, they are publicly charting individual targets and whether workers have reached their goals or not. The general manager at the plant says that this is the most difficult thing for American workers to adapt to when they start working for Toyota North America.

At first sight, it might seem that these highly visible demonstrations of individual success and failure is a way to show people up, but the objective, in fact, is to make problems visible and to enlist the help of colleagues if a worker is falling behind or needs support to find a solution. When the general manager joined the company ten years ago, she was shocked to find that the culture at Toyota was to expose problems in this way, especially to management. In the corporate environments she'd worked in previously, employees had always hidden problems from their bosses. However, now she was convinced that the Toyota way worked.

In order to maintain the Toyota values and to keep true to the original mission of winning customers with quality cars, Toyota has founded an institute responsible for developing executives for leadership positions. It is during this preparation that some of the most prized corporate secrets are instilled in the future leaders. The executives are then sent off around the world to different offices as missionaries, charged with the task of spreading the 'Toyota way of working'.

The general manager in charge of the Toyota institute is concerned and senses danger about the future as Toyota becomes increasingly global. He says that he fears the 'Toyota way' will be diluted by diverse cultural influences and working practices. In the past, the Toyota way was spread by word of mouth amongst Toyota's Japanese employees. However, as Toyota has expanded, it has been proved that these informal teaching methods alone are not enough to ensure the effective transfer of knowledge, so Toyota has moved to writing things down and making things more explicit. As a result, 'Toyota Institutes' have been set up, both in Japan and around the world, where practices are so confidential that no outsiders are permitted entrance. Key tenets include 'mutual ownership of problems', *genchi genbutsu* (solving problems at the source and not behind desks) and the *kaizen* mind (a constant sense of crisis which drives continuous improvement).

A former Toyota accountant from Tokyo says that if Toyota cannot infuse its philosophy into all its employees worldwide, quality problems will continue to occur. Today, only a third of Toyota's total workforce is employed at its Japanese plants, and executives say that its sprawling global operations do not always march to the same tune. Analysts warn that the biggest issue Toyota faces today is that the organisation is growing faster than its ability to transplant its culture to locations outside Japan. The founding of the 'Toyota Institute' is an attempt by the company to keep control and to manage growth, but it remains to be seen if this goal will be achieved.

a The coloured bar charts show the work targets of individual workers.
b Americans are used to making problems visible, according to the general manager.
c The Institute is very secretive.
d The Toyota Institute's main aim is to maintain the company's high health and safety standards around the world.
e The 'kaizen mind' is a way of solving problems at the source instead of behind desks.
f Toyota continues to ensure that the same quality standards are maintained across the world.

4 Do you think a corporate culture can be successfully taught in this way? Do you think Toyota is right to try to ensure that a single culture can operate across a wide range of countries?

Focus on language **5** Find a word or words in the article which mean the same as the following.
a tracking (paragraph 1)
b obtain (paragraph 2)
c established (paragraph 3)
d highly valued (paragraph 3)
e watered down (paragraph 4)
f spread out over a large area (paragraph 5)

6 The extract below is from a speech by the president of a company called Mirai in which he explains how they will establish a leadership training academy to support the future growth of the company. Complete the extract using words and phrases from the box.

> by word of mouth   developing   explicit
> infusing our philosophy   internationalisation   institution
> invest   keeping true   maintain   missionaries around the world
> our culture   teaching methods   to the same tune

'We believe that the only way to grow successfully is by **(a)** .... our people, to prepare them for **(b)** .... We will do this whilst **(c)** .... to our mission and by **(d)** .... into workers. Mirai has outgrown informal **(e)** .... , and we can no longer rely on transmitting our culture **(f)** .... We need to make our culture more **(g)** .... and get everyone marching **(h)** .... We will create an **(i)** .... and send off **(j)** .... to transplant **(k)** .... We must **(l)** .... in our people. In this way, we can **(m)** .... our company values, high-quality standards and top-class reputation in every market where we work.'

Let's talk **7** Work with a partner. In a recent staff survey, it was found that your company has a problem with poor motivation, due to there being a 'blame culture' (when individuals were blamed and held responsible for fixing problems). As a result, the senior management team has decided to create new company guidelines in this area. One of the guidelines is that 'there should be collective responsibility for problems, and solutions will be found together'.
You have trained some 'change leaders' who have now been sent out to each local office. Their job is to convince the local managers to take action to introduce and adopt the guidelines. Unfortunately, it's not going that well for Henric, one of the change leaders. His boss, David, has arranged a meeting with him to decide what they can do to turn things around.
Student A: Turn to page 89.
Student B: Turn to page 94.

6 Developing change leaders

D Intercultural competence: Developing change leaders across cultures

1 **Discuss these questions with a partner.**
   a How are leaders developed in your organisation?
   b Is feedback used as a way of encouraging or discouraging certain behaviour in your organisation?
   c How do you think giving and receiving feedback might differ across cultures? Can you give any examples from your own experience?

2 🎧 **33** Jean-Claude has just attended a meeting with his line manager, Petra, and other team members, including Ken. Listen to Jean-Claude reporting on the meeting to Pamela, a team member who wasn't present at the meeting, and answer these questions.
   a Why is Jean-Claude unhappy?
   b Why is Petra so customer-focused?
   c Why do you think Petra gives such direct feedback?
   d What does Pamela think about the way Petra gives feedback?
   e Why does Jean-Claude think Petra's feedback style is especially hard for Ken?
   f How do the team members decide to move forward?

3 When working internationally, it is very important to create common understanding about how to work together. During a team's formation, leaders should establish a culture in which the purpose and process of feedback is clear. This can be done by getting the team to collectively complete and commit to a set of agreed statements about feedback. Later, the team can compare what kind of culture they have with these earlier commitments.

> WHY: In our team, we believe that feedback is important because …
> (*It's important to clarify the positive purpose behind feedback.*)
>
> WHO: In our team, feedback should be given by …
> (*It's useful to clarify if feedback is top-down or bottom-up or both.*)
>
> WHEN/HOW: In our team, feedback should be given …
> (*This can mean: how frequently, in which medium – e.g. e-mail, face-to-face – and also whether it should be done one-to-one behind closed doors or in front of the whole group.*)
>
> WHAT NOT: In our team, feedback is not ….
> (*It's good to state what type of feedback to avoid.*)

With a partner, imagine you are working in an international team. Complete the sentences in the guidelines above using your own words, to define a team feedback culture which you would like to be part of. Then compare your ideas with another pair in the class, and agree which are the best sentences to describe an effective team feedback culture. Finally, read out your sentences in the class, getting and giving feedback on everyone's ideas.

Case study: Developing people through feedback internationally

Background Mike Kay leads a project team of HR professionals who are trying to create a standardised payroll system across their European organisation. Team members include the heads of HR from five countries: the UK (Mike), Germany (Paula Welz), Spain (Beatriz Sánchez), Italy (Silvio Macini) and Switzerland (Rudolf Steiner). The project has been running for six months and is expected to continue for another four months.

Situation Paula wants Mike to give some feedback to the team on their performance. She feels she has performed her role well and is really keen to get this kind of international experience. She wants to raise her profile in the organisation, so that she can be involved with bigger projects in future. She hopes this is recognised. However, during the project, she has become very frustrated with the slow progress, which she feels is due to:
- delays in decision-making (In Switzerland, Rudolf has spent a long time going over the details of the IT requirements and security needed for the new payroll system. This has delayed a decision on the IT specification.)
- other HR heads have promised to do things which, in fact, they haven't done. (In Spain, Beatriz promised to brief all staff involved with the new system to explain the changes taking place, but this is now a month overdue; in Italy, Silvio promised to liaise with all the HR heads to schedule staff training on the new system, but this hasn't been done yet.)

Paula spoke briefly to Mike at the end of the last face-to-face meeting in Milan, outlining the problems above. Mike promised to e-mail her about this, as he was in a hurry. The following e-mail from Mike arrives late in the evening (23:00) on Paula's return home to Germany.

> Hi Paula
> Good to see you at the recent meeting in Milan and great to hear that you are ready to go to Phase 2 of the project in Germany by the end of this month. I know you wanted some feedback. Nothing really very much to say other than keep up the good work!
> Regarding the other issues you mentioned, I'm sure they'll sort themselves out. Can you keep me informed of any problems which arise between now and the end of this phase?
> Best regards
> Mike

Paula didn't expect such a short response from the project leader. She decides to e-mail Mike the next day to communicate her dissatisfaction.

Tasks
1 **Discuss these questions with a partner.**
   a How effective is Mike's response to Paula's concerns?
   b Why do you think Paula reacted in the way she did to Mike's response?
   c What could Mike have done differently in his e-mail?

2 **You are a consultant who has been brought in to give feedback to Mike on his performance as project leader of the team. The project has stalled due to the issues that Paula has already identified, and you have found out the following information from discussions with the other team members (Silvio, Beatriz and Rudolf).**
   - Silvio has found out that Paula has criticised him directly to Mike. He is very angry, as he says he has already sent her an e-mail proposing a schedule of training for staff and he didn't get a response. Paula is adamant that she never got this e-mail.
   - Beatriz is unsure about how to write the document briefing the staff. She feels that her English isn't good enough and she feels insecure. She is delaying the task and is too afraid to ask for support.
   - Rudolf is complaining that Mike still hasn't approved the alterations needed to the IT specification to comply with Swiss rules on personal information security. Rudolf feels it is Mike's responsibility to finalise the specification for the whole programme.

   Discuss these questions in small groups.
   a What feedback could you give Mike on why the project has stalled?
   b How could Mike develop the skills of his team members to better handle the issues being described? What about his own leadership skills?
   c What actions should Mike take next?

3 **Present your answers to the other groups.**

6 Developing change leaders

E Language reference

Read through the key words and phrases below. Add any other useful words and expressions which you feel are important for you to learn. Make sure you find the time to review these words and phrases regularly and to use them at work.

Change management competences
Who are we? – team understanding
Where are we going? – direction
How do we plan to do it? – organisation
Who does what? – roles
What help is needed? – supporting people
How are we performing? – feedback
How are we seen in the organisation? – representing
Where are conflicts generated? – conflict
How are we co-operating as a team? – co-operation

Developing creativity and innovation
look at problems in creative ways
identify and understand different working and thinking styles
build on your strengths
compensate for weaknesses
stretch your thinking
consider ideas without judgement
empower the creativity of others
motivate people to innovate

Language for giving and receiving feedback
Could we review progress so far?
Could you tell me how you think things are going?
Yes, I can see that. / I've noticed that.
I've noticed that since the reorganisation, you've been working very hard to build a motivated team.
We really appreciate what you're doing to contribute to ...
Is there anything you think you could have done better?
This means that people are starting to change the way they do things.
... but maybe you could have given them more of your time.
I'd like to see you focus more on ...
What would you do differently next time?
If you'd spent more time supporting those who had to leave, do you think it could have helped?
What kind of support do you think would benefit you?
OK, so let's summarise the action points.

Language for training for change
delegate
assign
encourage
monitor
supervise
empower change agents as 'missionaries'
transplant culture
transmit culture by word of mouth
infuse a philosophy
instil management secrets
create an institute
prepare executives for leadership
alert co-workers and enlist their help in finding solutions
solve problems at the source instead of behind desk

Writing task Look at the Case study on pages 64–65. Draft an e-mail from Paula to Mike which gives feedback on Mike's e-mail and also requests a more detailed response in line with Paula's expectations. Then compare your answer with the one in the answer key (page 115).

F Change-management working tips and personal action plan

1 Take a few minutes to reflect on these tips on managing change which arise from this unit. How far do you agree with each one? Which do you think is the most important, and which ideas are the most useful?

TIP 1

In order to grow and develop, we need to be praised and motivated. We also need to learn from our mistakes and become aware of what we could do better. If we're not open to continuous improvement, how can we develop? This is why giving and receiving feedback is so important.

Ideas for giving feedback:
- Give positive feedback whenever you see behaviour which exemplifies the company values, goals and changes you want to see.
- Create a culture which doesn't focus on blame, but on constructive feedback with the aim of developing people and changing behaviours for the better.
- Think carefully about how you give the feedback and in what context.

TIP 2

Companies can set up leadership development and training programmes to try to infuse the desired values and behaviours into their people.

Ideas for creating leaders:
- Influence those around you or above you to implement change development.
- Change yourself: ask for feedback from others on what you could improve, and create your own action plan for change.

TIP 3

How should you give feedback? What should you give feedback on? Who should give feedback? Where and when should you give feedback? These are all questions to ask yourself and your team.

Ideas for tailoring feedback to culture:
- Establish a feedback culture which will both motivate and encourage everyone to develop.
- Focus on giving feedback about the behaviours associated with the change goals.
- Make sure team members are regularly asked for feedback and given feedback on their role in and progress of the project.
- After the project is finished, run a 'learning session', where everyone has the opportunity to give feedback on their experience in order to gather points for development and improvement next time.

Personal action plan 2 Take 15 minutes to review the unit. Write down at least three important points that you have learned and that you want to apply to your change-management practice. Then commit to a schedule to implement your learning and think about how you can check if you have been successful.

	what I have learned and want to apply in my change-management practice	when/how I will apply this in my change-management practice	how I will check if I have applied it
1			
2			
3			

7 Evaluating and measuring

AIMS
A To evaluate and measure change
B To ask SMART questions
C To monitor change through social media
D To measure success across cultures

A Discussion and listening

Think about it

> *What gets measured gets done.*
> Peter Drucker (1909–2005),
> American management consultant and author

1 When a company decides to implement change, what kind of things can be measured to discover whether the initiative is having the desired impact?

2 What experience have you had of measuring and evaluating change? What methods have you used?

Listen to this

3 🎧 **34** Hakon Johannsen works for a major paper company based in Sweden. Following a joint venture with a large forestry business in South America, Hakon has been asked to help with the integratation of the two organisations. Listen to the interview and answer these questions.
 a How did Hakon measure success?
 b Why does Hakon say it's important to involve a wide range of people when defining goals?
 c What kind of goal did Hakon decide to prioritise?
 d What example does Hakon give of a target that is easy to define?

4 🎧 **35** Listen to the next part of the interview and answer these questions.
 a What four things does Hakon say you can measure?
 b What was the most challenging thing to evaluate, according to Hakon?
 c What is Hakon's advice for dealing with ethical challenges?

5 Hakon says, 'The first objective of measuring change is to learn, and I repeat this every day: we learn from success and we learn even more from failure.' How much do you agree with this, and why?

Focus on language

6 Match each group of words (a–e) with the appropriate heading (1–5).

 1 People responsible
 2 Goal setting
 3 Methods of measurement
 4 Data
 5 Results of measurement

 a set/agree/define (goals/targets/objectives/milestones/deadlines/timeframes)
 b feedback surveys / observations / financial data / recorded interviews / social media (blogs, discussion groups)
 c succeed / fail / fall short of targets / more motivated staff / innovation
 d behaviour you can see / feedback you can hear / experiences you can feel / numbers you can count
 e stakeholders / consultants / top management / employees

7 Complete each of the phrases below from Tracks 34 and 35 with an appropriate verb from the box.

	blame	decide on	define	ensure	feel
	get	hide	measure	set	take

a .... success
b .... goals
c .... judged
d .... defensive
e .... mistakes
f .... others
g .... measures of success
h .... responsibility for fixing mistakes
i .... levels of ethical behaviour
j .... adherence to regulations

8 Complete the sentences below related to measuring change using the words from the box.

	adherence	commitment	compliance	filling
following	innovative	interviews	levels	motivation
	protection	qualitative	quantitative	reduction

a Set milestones for .... to new rules.
b Define deadlines for .... with guiding principles and practices.
c Agree targets for .... of workers' rights.
d You can measure whether employees are .... technical procedures.
e By using observation and data collected through recorded ...., you can check if there is a greater .... to sustainability.
f We wanted to set targets to increase the .... of ethical behaviour.
g Milestones can include things like successfully .... in records.
h Stakeholders need to agree to goals regarding .... of costs.
i One target we agreed to measure was related to creating more .... products.
j You can measure .... data like percentage increases in levels of staff .... based on feedback surveys, as well as .... results about how people feel gathered from social media platforms.

Let's talk

9 Your senior management has recently implemented a new set of guiding principles for leadership in the company. You and your team have the task of presenting a plan to department heads for evaluating levels of compliance with the principles. In groups of three or four, you need to plan how you will go about measuring this. Look at the brief below. Each group should prepare two of the guiding principles:

Group 1: guiding principles 1 and 2
Group 2: guiding principles 3 and 4
Group 3: guiding principles 5 and 6

Guiding principles
1 Be positive in communication.
2 Encourage a culture of constructive feedback to increase levels of performance.
3 Be supportive and motivate people.
4 Be demanding and expect high levels of efficiency.
5 Insist on the highest levels of ethical behaviour.
6 Contribute to a sustainable future.

Use these questions to help you structure your plan.
a Who will be involved?
b How will you set goals?
c How will you measure?
d What qualitative and quantitative data will you measure?
e What results do you hope to achieve?

Present your plan to the other groups.

7 Evaluating and measuring

B Communication skills: Asking SMART questions

Think about it 1 What experience do you have of goal-setting? What sort of goals are set in your company? Who sets them?

2 Are you familiar with SMART objectives? Do you know what the letters stand for?

Listen to this 3 🎧 36 Saheed, a change manager, is talking to a group of leaders who will be responsible for implementing change in their company. Listen to his presentation and answer these questions.

> a What makes a goal **specific**?
>
> b How does **measurable** progress help a team?
>
> c What three things should you be able to develop to make a goal **achievable**?
>
> d Why do goals need to be **relevant** to your boss, team and organisation?
>
> e Why are **time-bound** goals so important during a change initiative?

4 Do you think this method is or could be successful in your working context? Why? / Why not?

5 Read the extracts below from Track 36. What kind of goals is the speaker referring to in each case? Match each extract with one of the SMART objectives (in bold in Exercise 3).
  a This stresses the importance of goals that are realistic and attainable. You should be able to develop the attitudes, skills and financial capacity to reach them.
  b This stresses the importance of choosing goals that matter. Many times, you'll need support to accomplish a goal: resources, a champion, someone to remove obstacles.
  c This means the goal is clear and unambiguous … [Goals] must tell a team exactly what's expected, why it's important, who's involved, and where it's going to happen.
  d It's key to set goals within a time frame, giving them a target date. A commitment to a deadline helps a team focus its efforts on completion of the goal on or before the due date.
  e [This] is supposed to help a team stay on track, reach its target dates and experience the sense of achievement that motivates it to put in the continued effort required to reach the ultimate goal.

Focus on language

6 Put the words into the correct order to make questions.

a will / how / successful / you / if / are / know / you / ?
b to / success / in / does / goal / mean / what / relation / this / ?
c success / people / to / does / mean / different / what / ?
d measure / can / what / you / ?
e realistic / the / goals / are / ?
f possible / all / obstacles / you / have / considered / the / ?
g goals / are / organisation / to / relevant / your / the / ?
h that / support / receive / needed / you / will / ?
i will / deadlines / what / set / milestones and / you / ?

> **Tip**
> It is very useful to ask questions when evaluating the results of a change effort.

7 Complete the questions below using the words from the box.

| exactly | hindsight | reflection | retrospect | think | would |

a In ...., what needed to be adapted in the plan?
b Do you .... the actions agreed to achieve the goals had the desired impact?
c On ...., which actions were not so relevant and could have been stopped?
d .... you say that goals achieved had a positive impact on all the people involved?
e How .... did you decide which milestones to set?
f With the benefit of ...., what would you have done differently?

Let's talk

8 a Tell a partner about a change story. Spend a few minutes planning your story. It might help to use SMART to present it. Look at the questions below to help you.

b Ask questions about your partner's story and answer their questions about yours.

Specific	• What were the change goals? • What did you want to accomplish, and what were the benefits of accomplishing those goals? • Who was involved?
Measurable	• How would you know if you were successful? • What did success mean in relation to this project/goal? • What did success mean to different people? • How did you measure both positive and negative impact of change?
Achievable	• Were the goals realistic? • Had you considered all the possible obstacles? • In retrospect, what needed to be adapted in the plan?
Relevant	• Did you have support? • Do you think the actions agreed to achieve the goals had the desired impact? • On reflection, which actions were not so relevant and could have been stopped? • Would you say that goals achieved had a positive impact on all the people involved?
Time-bound	• How exactly did you decide which milestones to set? • What was the timescale to achieve aims? • Did you achieve your aims?

7 Evaluating and measuring

C Professional skills: Monitoring change through social media

Think about it   **1** What kinds of social media do you use, and for what purpose?

2 One of the most difficult things to measure in change programmes is how people feel. Do you think that social media can be an effective means of monitoring this? What is your experience?

Read this   **3** Read the article on page 73 and match each of these headings (1–4) to a paragraph (A–D).
1 Establishing more effective two-way communication
2 Sharing current practices through a knowledge network
3 Assessing progress more regularly and effectively
4 Building a collaborative culture

4 Answer these questions about the article.
a What has employee feedback shown about changes in the organisational structure at USTRANSCOM since the introduction of social-media programmes?
b How can managers identify any problems employees may be experiencing in change programmes?
c How can messaging services and social-networking platforms help change programmes to succeed by sharing new ways of doing things?
d What is the main advantage of using survey-based and facilitated online feedback sessions when monitoring change programmes?

Focus on language   **5** Complete this summary about the benefits of social media for measuring change using relevant words or phrases from the article.
Since USTRANSCOM launched several social-media initiatives, including an executive blog, a Q&A blog and a public presence on Facebook and Twitter, social-media platforms have:
a helped where creating a more .... is one of the objective of the change initiative
b flattened the organisational ....
c driven positive ....
d provided an effective ....
Management can:
e see where any misunderstanding or .... exist across the enterprise and take steps to address them
f establish a .... for delivering the 'voice of truth' – an authoritative, trusted and believable source of information
g get near .... about how well a programme is going
h have .... about employees' understanding and acceptance of the change programme.
Social-media platforms can help employees:
i form .... using applications such as Twitter, Yammer and Facebook
j get information about new processes or technologies, share .... and receive answers in timely ways.

Let's talk   **6** The authors mention more positives than negatives regarding the use of social media for monitoring change. Can you think of any other disadvantages of using these methods? Do you think the ideas mentioned in the article would work in the same way in your country? Discuss as a group.

Ways in which social media can accelerate large-scale change

by Mohsin Ghafoor and Trinity Martin

Introduction
According to numerous studies, anywhere from 50 percent to 80 percent of change programs do not live up to expectations. Although the reasons for failure vary, many can be traced to the difficulty with managing multiple organizational elements effectively across a global enterprise—creating a shared vision, gaining buy-in across locations and levels, dealing with expectations, and handling the day-to-day upheavals inherent in change. Accenture believes that these challenges are well suited to the capabilities of social media and collaboration tools.

A
Social media can help in cases where creating a more collaborative culture is one of the major objectives of the change initiative. This has been the case with the United States Transportation Command, or USTRANSCOM. Executives sought to change the structure and culture of USTRANSCOM from a "command and control" emphasis to one that encouraged staff to interact directly with executives and supported the kinds of collaboration that can lead to innovation. USTRANSCOM launched several social-media initiatives, including an executive blog and a Q&A blog hosted on the Command's intranet, as well as a public presence on Facebook and Twitter. The executive blog (which has been recognized by the U.S. Department of Defense as a best practice) enables executives to hear from staff directly, without having messages filtered through intermediate management levels. These social-media programs have flattened the organizational hierarchy and driven positive culture shifts, as measured by an annual staff survey.

B
Social-media tools provide an effective communications medium—for the core change program teams and across the organization as a whole—as a large-scale change initiative proceeds. In addition, by monitoring and participating in online discussions, managers can more readily see where any misunderstandings or "pain points" exist across the enterprise and take steps to address them. Participation by leadership in social-media-based collaboration platforms is essential. Collaboration tools can actually undermine change effectiveness if they merely cause confusion and discontent to multiply across social networking sites. Management must establish a mechanism for delivering the "voice of truth"—an authoritative, trusted, and believable source of information. This reinforces the idea that social media can be used by employees not only to voice ideas and concerns but also to get accurate and credible answers regarding the company's change effort.

C
"Learning" refers to more than just the formal offerings that are designed and delivered from a central group. Also critical are the knowledge networks that can be formed quickly using applications such as Twitter, Yammer, and Facebook. These networks can help employees get information about new processes or technologies, share innovative practices, and receive answers in timely ways.

D
How do organizations know whether they are making progress on a large-scale change program from an employee perspective? Enterprises sometimes have difficulty measuring progress, but social-media applications can help by providing near real-time feedback about how well a program is going. Assessments can be supported in at least two ways: by providing a platform for nearly instantaneous survey-based feedback, which can supplement more comprehensive measurement exercises; and by conducting facilitated online feedback sessions. With social-media tools, decision makers have timely information about employees' understanding and acceptance of the change program.

adapted from www.accenture.com

D Intercultural competence: Measuring success across cultures

1 Read this extract from the end-of-year intranet message from Martin Benn, the CEO of a large electronics retailer. Which two changes to his company's culture does he want to see in the following year?

> We have been successful with a very decentralised organisation. In the past, people were encouraged to act on their own initiative. All of our stores operated independently. Each country did things in its own way for its local customers. But we need to change. The marketplace is more global today, and we have to internationalise. This means more IT centralisation – standardising and harmonising our IT infrastructure across different countries, for example. It also means more focus on innovation – taking the best from single countries and passing great ideas around the group. In order to achieve our targets, we require much more co-operation across borders – acting much more together as a global company, rather than alone as national operations. It's complex, so we need to measure and track the success of these changes.

2 Martin says that the company needs 'to measure and track the success of these changes'. In what ways do you think a company can measure the success of the changes that he is proposing?

3 Read the second part of Martin's message and answer the questions below.

> So far, we can report that we have achieved 80% of our 'centralisation of IT' targets, which means we've cut the number of operating systems from 35 to 18 globally. We believe that the decision to centrally fund the project has contributed to our success. Concerning innovation, in some countries we are facing resistance to the transfer of best practice from one country to another. This is happening particularly in the more mature, risk-averse markets. As a result, we are only 33% towards our goal, with two big projects running rather than our objective of six. If we're going to be successful in future, we have to take risks, be more flexible and build trust across our borders. Having said that, it's important to celebrate the success stories. A good example of this is the after-sales collaboration programme led by the US electronics division. Sharing ideas, solutions and best practice has resulted in a faster and more efficient response to customer complaints. According to surveys, customers feel that our service has improved by 65%, and over 80% of customers said that they would buy from us again, an average increase of 30% on previous national surveys. This is what we want to see, drawing on all our global expertise to gain competitive advantage.

a Why do you think the company has had more success so far with the IT centralisation programme than the innovation project?
b How does the company measure the success of the innovation project described?
c What does Martin mention as an important success factor for the company?

4 a Imagine you are the CEO of your organisation. Think about one element of your own organisational culture which you would like to change to support international working. Prepare a short presentation describing:
- what the change is
- why the change is important
- what is needed to manage any cultural problems connected to the change
- how you would propose to measure the success of the change.

b Form small groups and make a short presentation of your idea, answering any questions. After all the presentations, vote for the best idea.

Case study: Changing project management

Background Santek Industries is a US-based global leader in the manufacture of specialist components for the automotive industry. A recent internal analysis revealed that it has wasted over $1bn on projects in the last three years. The figures are clear:
- 23% of projects failed totally
- 55% of projects ran significantly over budget
- 73% of projects were completed late.

In response, Santek's central project management office in Boston plans to introduce a new project management system across its global operations based on PMI, which is a global standard. The change for those running projects in local markets will be significant, as everyone is using different standards.

Situation Ron Pacini is head of the project office at the Canadian subsidiary of Santek Industries. He is responsible for leading three major projects himself and supervises ten other projects running nationally. He has just received the following e-mail from Fabio Berg, Head of Project Planning in Boston.

> Dear Ron
>
> It was good to meet with you at the recent leadership meeting. As you heard, we are planning to change our project management methodology across the company as of January 1 next year.
>
> This will require that all those running or responsible for national projects should change a number of key areas of their work:
> - apply a new project-planning and risk-analysis methodology
> - report monthly to me on the status of national projects
> - request authorization from me (rather than from the local CEO) for any additional spending.
>
> We will also publish on our intranet a set of metrics to show how far projects are on track in terms of cost, time, and scope, as we believe greater visibility will help to ensure greater professionalism across the company.
>
> Further information will be available at our next conference call at the end of the week.
>
> Regards
> Fabio

Tasks

1 Discuss these questions.
   a How do you think Ron might respond to this e-mail?
   b How do you think he *should* respond? Why?

2 🎧 37 Listen to a telephone call between Ron and Susan Krabbe, a colleague in Germany, about the e-mail from Fabio.
   a What is the main thing that Ron dislikes about the message from Fabio?
   b What does he say is 'logistically impossible'? Why?
   c How far does Susan agree with Ron? Why?
   d Why does Ron say that Fabio's proposals 'don't make sense'?

3 How far do you agree with Ron's arguments? Why?

4 a With a partner, prepare a short presentation which Ron can give to Fabio at their next meeting. Firstly, decide how far you want the presentation to support or argue against the planned change (and why). Structure your presentation by explaining the main advantages and disadvantages of the planned change in project management methodology and the measures to track success. At the end of the presentation, give some recommendations for next steps.

   b Work with another pair and give your presentations to each other. Get feedback on how effective people think your presentation would be in front of Fabio.

E Language reference

Read through the key words and phrases below. Add any other useful words and expressions which you feel are important for you to learn. Make sure you find the time to review these words and phrases regularly and to use them at work.

Evaluating and measuring terms
measure = evaluate / assess / monitor / track progress
set = agree / define / specify
goals = targets / objectives / milestones / deadlines / time frames
fail = fall short of targets
make corrections = adapt goals
commit to (v) / commitment (n)
protect (v) / protection (n)
adhere to (v) / adherence (n)
comply with (v) / compliance (n)
reduce (v) / reduction (n)
motivate (v) / motivation (n)
fill in (forms, etc.)
follow (rules/regulations, etc.)

Evaluating and measuring questions
Are the goals realistic?
What does success mean in relation to this goal?
What can you measure?
How will you know if you are successful?
Have you considered all the possible obstacles?
What were the change goals?
What were the benefits of accomplishing the goals?
Who was involved?
What did you want to accomplish?
How would you know if you were successful?
Had you considered all the possible obstacles?
What would you have done differently?

Project terms
global project portfolio
project management office
standardised project management framework
American standard / global standard.
project management methodology
to run/lead/supervise projects
to report on the status of a project
to apply project-planning and risk-analysis methodology
metrics: cost/time/scope
on track
over budget
waste money

Writing task Write a PowerPoint slide defining SMART objectives for a project that you are working on or a project you are planning.

F Change-management working tips and personal action plan

1 Take a few minutes to reflect on these tips on managing change which arise from this unit. How far do you agree with each one? Which do you think is the most important, and which ideas are the most useful?

TIP 1

It's important that you have a respected and representative group of stakeholders before you set change goals.
Ideas for assessing stakeholders' views:
- Listen to a diverse range of views before deciding what and how to measure.
- Take into account different functional and cultural perspectives.
- Make sure you have enough key people on board who have the ability to drive change goals successfully and to achieve targets, but with the awareness that it is also necessary to be flexible regarding how those goals are achieved.

TIP 2

Measure a balance of data: quantitative (numbers and hard data) and qualitative (observable changes in behaviour, feedback from people on how they feel, etc.).
Ideas for using data:
- Set SMART goals (Specific, Measureable, Achievable, Relevant, Time-bound) and set regular milestones to reinforce short-term wins.
- When you have completed each stage, evaluate how effective the process has been and make any necessary adjustments.
- Evaluate acceptance of change and how people feel about it by using a mix of social-media tools, online discussion forums, feedback and surveys, anonymous feedback channels which can be done on a more global level, and personal interviews done on a local level.

TIP 3

Many people gain more satisfaction and motivation from achieving targets when their successes are recognised. In complex change projects, results can take time to emerge, and much persistence and determination is required to keep the momentum going.
Ideas for keeping up momentum:
- Make sure you set a range of goals relevant to all parts of the business, in all countries.
- Build in flexibility to your goals when working in an unfamiliar context.
- Break any change targets into small steps and celebrate each success as it happens; communicate this widely and recognise and reward those who were responsible for the achievement in an appropriate way for each cultural context. In this way, those who resist change may be encouraged to engage more actively.

Personal action plan 2 Take 15 minutes to review the unit. Write down at least three important points that you have learned and that you want to apply to your change-management practice. Then commit to a schedule to implement your learning and think about how you can check if you have been successful.

	what I have learned and want to apply in my change-management practice	when/how I will apply this in my change-management practice	how I will check if I have applied it
1			
2			
3			

7 Evaluating and measuring

8 Cultural shifts

AIMS
A To consider what helps change to last
B To present arguments
C To change business culture
D To build diverse teams

A Discussion and listening

Think about it

> *Nothing endures but change.*
> Heraclitus (540 BC–480 BC),
> Greek philosopher

1 Think about a change experience you've been through. How long did it take you to get used to the change? How or why did you get used to it in the end?

2 In your opinion, what needs to happen in order to get change to last? Do you think change ever remains for long?

Listen to this

3 🎧 38 Etsuko Oshiro, HR Director for a major sports equipment brand, is talking about the challenges of getting major change to last. Listen to the interview and answer these questions.
 a How long has it taken Etsuko's company to achieve the goals of the change programme?
 b What barrier to change did the CEO face early on in the change process?
 c How is Etsuko different from the original management team in her company?
 d What was Etsuko brought in to do as part of the company change programme?

4 🎧 39 Listen to the second part of the interview and answer these questions.
 a What needed to be in place to support the changes in working practice?
 b When did Etsuko eventually see change happen?
 c What message is important to get to workers whilst change is in progress?
 d What two things need to happen to consolidate change?

Focus on language

5 Complete the advice below on consolidating change using the verbs from the box.

| allow | change | demonstrate | go through | look for | rethink |

You have to:
a .... time for change to become established.
b .... a process of transformation / all the steps.
c .... positive results.
d .... attitudes and practices.
e .... learning opportunities.
f continually .... the needs of the business.

6 Complete the summary below using the words and phrases from the box.

> autonomy   company-wide training programmes
> compatible with diversity goals   different perspectives   diverse workforce
> employee rotation   family-friendly policies   jobs and family   take risks

To build a creative and (a) .... , you need to bring in people with (b) .... It's important to set up (c) .... to enable women to balance (d) .... To encourage diversity in your team, you can put in place (e) .... In addition, to foster creativity, you should encourage people to (f) .... and give employees more (g) .... To disseminate new ways of working and share ideas, you can introduce (h) .... Finally, it's essential to make reward and promotion policies (i) ....

7 a Are you a creative thinker? How do you think when you are looking for ideas and solutions? Circle the words that predominantly apply to your way of thinking.

logical   objective   intuitive   impulsive   holistic   planned   free
specific   imaginative   emotional   focus on qualitative data   realistic
focus on quantitative data   subjective   intellectual   structured

b Look at the key (page 116) to see if you are a more creative or a more analytical thinker. Compare your answers with the rest of the group. Are there more creative or more analytical thinkers?

Let's talk **8 What do you do as a team to encourage creativity? What methods do you have in place to challenge convention and encourage different ways of thinking?**

9 Try this brainstorming activity to practise innovative, creative thinking.

> Present a problem you are having at work to the group. Tell the group why it is a problem, what you have already tried and the possible consequences if you can't resolve it.
> Try a collaborative approach – gather possible solutions from the group and get a range of views. Ask each person then to consider what might happen if you did the opposite.
>
> For the rest of the group, try:
> - reframing the problem: Is it really a problem? How could you make a positive out of a negative?
> - asking questions about the people involved in/around the problem: Do you really know who they are / what they want / what their priorities are? Who could help, and how?
> - asking about what has already been tried: What exactly caused it to fail? Is it worth trying this approach again, but adapting it / changing something?
>
> Put all your thoughts on a flipchart and decide on three possible solutions to the issue.
>
> 'This collaboration would work better if you kept your ideas to yourself.'

8 Cultural shifts

B Communication skills: Presenting arguments

Think about it

1 Think of a speaker who inspires you. Who are they, and why are they inspirational?

2 What are the important points to consider when presenting an argument or giving a speech?

Listen to this

3 Aristotle introduced a model for arguing a case that describes how we need to balance three elements when presenting an argument:
   1 logos (influencing through reason)
   2 ethos (influencing through credibility)
   3 pathos (influencing through emotion)

   Match each element (1–3) with its definition (a–c).
   a People are influenced because you draw on shared values, beliefs and fears to connect with people emotionally.
   b People are influenced because you present a clear, honest, authoritative position, showing evidence and examples of experience.
   c People are influenced because you provide evidence, facts and examples to build a logical case.

4 🎧 **40–42** Listen to Dr Roberto Takamoto, a member of the United Nations environmental team, presenting the case for a cultural shift in the way business thinks about sustainability. His presentation is in three sections (1–3). Listen to each one and decide which of the three elements from Exercise 3 (logos, ethos or pathos) Dr Takamoto is mainly focusing on.

5 a 🎧 **40–42** Listen to the presentation again. Divide into three groups. Each group should focus on a different section (1–3). Note down some key information from your section. Complete these notes to help you as you listen.

'What if we don't change at all ... and something magical just happens?'

> **Section 1**
> Good afternoon, my name is ... and I work for ...
> Before that, I was ... and was responsible for ...
> I have worked in ...
>
> **Section 2**
> I'd like to start by ...
> We're facing three key challenges: ...
> These three factors combined mean we're ...
> Between ... and .... by 33% ...
> Many companies see longer-term sustainability as a key driver of ...
> For example, ...
>
> **Section 3**
> If we don't ... , ... will ...
> Ask yourself this: How can I ...?
> I think you'll find the answer lies in ...

b Now form new groups of three. Each group should include one member from each of the original groups. Together, rebuild the presentation. Present your version to the class and ask for feedback on how convincing you are.

8 Cultural shifts

Focus on language **6** Decide whether each of these words and phrases is used to add information or contrast and add them to the table below.

~~although~~	~~as well as~~	contrary to	despite	furthermore
however	in addition	like	nevertheless	on the other hand
similarly	unless	unlike	whereas

addition	contrast
as well as	although

7 Complete each of these sentences with a suitable word or phrase from Exercise 6. In some cases, more than one answer is possible.
 a Anglo-Saxon business culture tends to focus on short-term gain. .... , this does not ensure sustainable long-term success.
 b Sustainability strategies will not be successful .... employees are engaged.
 c Communicating a company's vision for change successfully is a key factor. .... , it's important to actively involve people at every level.
 d .... sustainable business practice being important for the future, many companies are not changing the way they do things.
 e .... in previous centuries, workers' rights and welfare around the world are now more important to consumers, signalling a change in attitudes.

8 Influencing people to change by connecting with their emotions can have a more lasting impact. Match each of these phrases (a–r) to one of the four ways below (1–4) in which you can do this. Some phrases may relate to more than one way.

 a If we don't change now, …
 b I'd like you to picture the following scenario.
 c I think you've all seen your bonuses reduce.
 d What do you see?
 e Do you remember last summer? There was no rain …
 f How would you feel if …?
 g What would it feel like if …?
 h Imagine this …
 i We can't afford to wait.
 j Let me describe the future that I see.
 k All of our energy bills are increasing.
 l This is about you.
 m Ask yourself this … how can we?
 n What about your family?
 o It's now or never.
 p It's not too late to change your mind.
 q Over 80% of our employees are benefiting from our new family policy.
 r What legacy will I leave …?

 1 Create urgency
 2 Visualise / Help people see the message
 3 Give real examples to illustrate
 4 Be personal / Connect to people's own experiences

> 'People change what they do less because they are given analysis that shifts their thinking, than because they are shown a truth that influences their feelings.'
> www.kotterinternational.com

Let's talk **9** With a partner, imagine you are implementing a sustainability strategy. As you can only demonstrate the positive results of your strategy over time, it's essential that you try to change attitudes now. Look at the notes on page 90, then prepare a speech to give to the rest of the group. Try to use as much of the language from this section as possible.

8 Cultural shifts

C Professional skills: Changing business culture

Think about it

1 How has the nature of the workforce changed since you started working? (Think about nationality, gender, age, etc.)

2 What policies, if any, are in place to encourage women to enter the workforce and develop their careers?

Read this

3 Read this article and answer the questions on page 83.

Changing the corporate culture: Microsoft reaps the rewards of female managers
by Michaela Schiessl

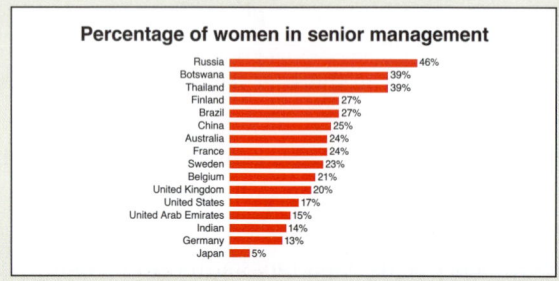

Percentage of women in senior management

Country	%
Russia	46%
Botswana	39%
Thailand	39%
Finland	27%
Brazil	27%
China	25%
Australia	24%
France	24%
Sweden	23%
Belgium	21%
United Kingdom	20%
United States	17%
United Arab Emirates	15%
Indian	14%
Germany	13%
Japan	5%

Grant Thornton IBR 2012

Women rarely make it into senior management in German corporations, but Microsoft Germany is now setting an example of how to systematically achieve equality for women. Shrinking populations in Europe are forcing companies to get serious about bringing women into the executive leagues. It's a step that is also helping them become more profitable.

The US women's organisation Catalyst examined the 500 biggest corporations in America and came to the same conclusion as the relatively unbiased corporate consulting firm McKinsey: companies with a blend of male and female senior executives are more successful, both economically and in terms of their corporate culture. According to the studies, the companies with the most women in senior management achieved a return on equity that was up to 53 per cent higher than those without women in top-ranking positions.

'Diversity is extremely important,' says Achim Berg, the general manager of Microsoft Germany. 'Diversity begets quality.' A former member of the executive board of T-Com, Berg resigned in early 2007 to assume his current position at Microsoft Germany – and found that there were already three female directors on the board. He appointed two more, so that there are now five women on the company's 13-member management board – an exception in the German business world. When he reveals that all five female senior executives are also mothers of young children, he manages to upset quite a few established views of the way things work in business.

It has since become clear that corporate Germany needs women. But recruiting them is easier said than done. 'A family-friendly environment is the killer criterion for women. If it isn't what they want, we don't get them,' says Microsoft's Director of Human Resources Brigitte Hirl-Höfer, who has gone to great lengths to create an attractive environment so that she can recruit the best talent. Microsoft organises and helps pay for daycare centres, operates a parents' and babysitters' exchange and pays agency fees for all kinds of family services, from babysitting to care for the elderly. Job solutions are customised for women returning to work after maternity leave. The company provides technical equipment for those employees who wish to work at home, and employees on maternity or paternity leave are copied in on important documents to keep them in the loop.

But there is one condition that must be met for all of these programmes to work, explains Hirl-Höfer: 'The culture of flexible working hours must have strong acceptance.' The magic phrase at Microsoft's third-largest subsidiary outside the United States is 'trust-based working hours', and it has helped the company to not only achieve strong returns but has repeatedly earned it the distinction of being voted Germany's most popular employer. 'We agree to certain goals with each employee. How and where they are reached is secondary,' says Hirl-Höfer. As refreshingly simple and uncomplicated as this sounds, it remains a distant goal for many companies, say the authors of a McKinsey study entitled 'Women matter'. In most cases, the rules of professional life are tailored to men whose wives stay at home to run the household and raise their children. For instance, the notion that it should be possible to send an employee anywhere at any time is incompatible with the double burden women face. Mothers, in particular, are unable to satisfy corporate demands for their undivided attention. 'As long as the criteria for promotion are not changed, little will change in the situation of women in leadership positions,' the McKinsey study concludes.

At Microsoft, the new way of thinking begins at the bottom. The company gives preferential treatment in the hiring process to women with the same qualifications as men applying for the same positions, and women already make up 28 per cent of the company's 2,200 employees. At Microsoft, each employee receives a performance review twice a year, and employees also evaluate their supervisors. Supervisors, in turn, are asked to pay special attention to recruiting new female employees and to consider female candidates when filling existing positions. Acceptance among senior executives is one of the most important criteria for achieving equal treatment of women in the corporate world. McKinsey warns that nothing will change unless management actively supports and aggressively promotes the goal of promoting women managers.

adapted from www.spiegel.de

a What conclusion did Catalyst and McKinsey come to about firms that have a mix of men and women in senior management?
b What is unconventional about the profile of some of the senior management at Microsoft Germany?
c What does Brigitte Hirl-Höfer think is necessary for a workplace to have in order to attract women?
d Why is Microsoft Germany considered to be such a good place to work?
e What is the problem that mothers have with the expected norms of work?
f How do Microsoft's recruitment procedures support equality?
g According to McKinsey, what needs to change in business culture for women to become more equal to men in the workplace?

Focus on language

4 Find the words and phrases in the article that mean the same as these expressions.
a a balance of men and women managers
b working practices that enable parents to have children and manage their jobs
c to make sure [people] have information
d not in line with
e a bias in favour of
f appraisal

5 Complete each gap in the pieces of advice below using the correct form of one of the words from the box. One word is used twice.

| customise | employ | equip | perform | prefer |
| promote | recruit | supervise | treat | |

What can be done to change the male-dominated culture of the corporate world?
a Have regular .... reviews with women employees.
b Ask women to evaluate their ....
c Give .... to women in the hiring process.
d Pay special attention to .... new female employees.
e Encourage senior executives to .... women equally.
f Introduce the goal of .... women managers.
g .... job solutions for women returning to work after maternity leave.
h Provide technical .... for those employees who wish to work at home.
i Copy in .... on maternity or paternity leave on important documents to keep them in the loop.

Let's talk

6 Ask a partner these questions.
a What percentage of women is there in your company workforce?
b What percentage of women is there in your company management?
c Are there any policies in place that promote women entering the company and progressing up the career ladder?
d What family-friendly policies or facilities are there in your company?
e Have you ever had a female manager? What was your experience?
f What needs to change in your company to increase the number of women in management?
g Do you think there should be (more) women managers in your company? Why? / Why not?

8 Cultural shifts

83

D Intercultural competence: Building diverse teams

1 How culturally diverse is the company you work for / your team?

2 Does your company actively promote international working / cross-cultural teamwork? Why? / Why not?

3 How far do you agree with these statements?

a Strong company cultures with one predominant national group are hard to change.

b The turbulent world today requires companies that are flexible and continually learning.

c Leaders should stimulate diversity in their management and in their teams.

d The most culturally diverse organisations will be better prepared to deal with unpredictable events.

e Building good cross-cultural communication and understanding is an essential task for leaders.

4 Martha Pender is a manager in a technology company in the oil industry. She is responsible for building a new global innovation team. This is the first time she has managed a diverse team, so this is a big change for her. She has built up an international group of people with great talents and she's excited about the results they could achieve. Recently, she gave the team a number of technical problems they needed to solve. She told them to come to a brainstorming meeting with ideas. However, since that meeting, communications have broken down between team members. Martha has spoken to the people involved to find what went wrong.

🎧 43–46 Listen to excerpts from her meetings with four of the team. Match each of the speakers (1–4) with these guidelines for managing diverse teams (a–d).

a Before having any formal meetings, agree with the team members guidelines for what meetings you will have and what expectations each member has about these different types of meeting.

b Define what you mean by 'brainstorming' and consider all cultural perspectives. Some cultures can be sensitive to people questioning and challenging their ideas in a meeting context, especially if challenges are personalised.

c Agree in advance a clear purpose for each meeting, with a clear time to start and finish. If you want the meeting to be less formal and structured, make it clear what you intend to achieve and by when.

d Learn about different communication styles and cultural preferences. Some cultures prefer not to bring conflicts or problems to the surface. Be sensitive if people don't want to talk about a problem.

5 How do you think Martha could make sure that her team will produce good results and be effective in the longer term?

Case study: Candidate selection

Background Packup is a traditional company producing plastic and cardboard packaging for the retail market. The company is mostly based in the UK. The workforce is not very diverse, and all of the management is male. Recently, large customers have been putting pressure on companies like Packup to come up with better, cheaper packaging solutions.

Situation Richard Gray, the company's founder and owner, is nearing retirement and is very concerned about the future of the business. Although it's been very successful in the past, he feels it needs more diversity as part of its leadership team for the future.

Tasks

1 Richard Gray has appointed you as recruitment consultants to help him to find the next leader of the company. He wants a person with a fresh perspective to develop new products which will be more innovative, sustainable and therefore successful in the future. Look at Richard's criteria, in order of priority (1 = most important):
  1 Ideally appoint a woman to this position, as there are no women in the management team currently.
  2 The next generation of products should be sold more globally, so ideally the candidate should have international marketing experience, especially in Asia.
  3 The person needs to be entrepreneurial and to think outside the box.
  4 They need to have a strong interest in and knowledge of sustainable business practice.
  5 They will need strong leadership and motivational skills.
  6 They don't necessarily need a technical background, as the business has an excellent R&D team, but some technical experience would be an advantage.

2 There is a shortlist of three candidates for the new job. Work in groups of three. Each person looks at one candidate profile and matches that person against the criteria, making notes on their suitability.
  Student A: See below.
  Student B: Turn to page 94.
  Student C: Turn to page 95.

> **Student A**
> **Candidate: Maria**
> Maria lives in the UK. She is 29 years old and she has two children at school. She has a Master's in management and marketing; her thesis was on 'marketing the idea of reusing and recycling'. She has been working for four years as a team leader in waste management in local government (with a small team of six). Her main achievement has been to significantly increase corporate engagement with major waste reduction and recycling programmes. She is passionate about reducing waste and has inspired her team, some of whom have recently been made redundant. She no longer feels motivated to stay and is looking for a more challenging position. Maria has never worked abroad, but her mother is from Poland. She speaks Polish, as well as English and some German.

3 Meet as a group and discuss the suitability of your candidate for the job. Listen to the other presentations, ask and answer questions and then decide together which candidate is in fact the best person to appoint.

8 Cultural shifts

E Language reference

Read through the key words and phrases below. Add any other useful words and expressions which you feel are important for you to learn. Make sure you find the time to review these words and phrases regularly and to use them at work.

Creativity/diversity language
diverse workforce
different perspectives
to take risks
family-friendly policies
jobs and family
employee rotation
autonomy
company-wide training programmes
compatible with diversity goals

Language for giving a speech
I was a senior executive in … / I have worked in …
I have … years of experience of …
I can tell you some success stories; for example, …
I have been a visiting lecturer at …
I have a degree in …
I have done research in …
I have written a book about …
Sales reached 18 billion dollars in 2012.
The company predicts revenue growth of €120m by 2015.
Profits increased/rose by 15%.
Staff turnover reduced by 8%.
We saw staff motivation rise by 3%.
We saved 50,000 euros in 2013.
If we don't change now, … will …

Asking rhetorical questions
How can we meet this demand and guarantee sustainability?
Ask yourself this: 'How can I ensure the future success of my company, and what legacy will I leave for the next generations?'

Contrast
Although some are still focused on short-term gain, many companies see longer-term sustainability as a key driver of innovation and change.

Using emotive language, metaphor and simile
But if we don't change now …
I think you'll find the answer lies in …

The rule of three
We are facing three key challenges: …

Women and equality
to appoint women to management boards
female senior executives
family-friendly working environment
to recruit the best talent
daycare centres / babysitters' exchange
maternity/paternity leave
flexible working hours
equal treatment of women / gender equality
to promote/encourage/empower women

Writing task Think about a change project that you are or your company is working on. Consider key reasons why this change is important in the long term. Write an inspirational speech to change people's attitudes, using as many techniques described in the unit as possible.

F Change-management working tips and personal action plan

1 Take a few minutes to reflect on these tips on managing change which arise from this unit. How far do you agree with each one? Which do you think is the most important, and which ideas are the most useful?

TIP 1

In order to make change stick, top management has to be committed; you have to work through all the necessary steps with patience and persistence and you have to show positive results to the stakeholders.

Ideas for making change stick:
- Move away from a rigid company structure to a more flexible environment.
- Promote creativity by encouraging brainstorming and channeling any innovative ideas that come out into projects. A diverse, creative group of people is more likely to adapt to change and to continue adapting in future.

TIP 2

If you want people to accept change in the longer term, you need to convince them that what you are doing is the right thing.

Ideas for persuasion:
- When presenting your case, use evidence of your experience and authenticity, logical reasoning, facts and examples – and connect with people on an emotional level. Remember that it's important to influence 'the heart' if you want to change attitudes more fundamentally.
- Make sure you find out what is really important to people and speak to them in relation to this.

TIP 3

Having a balance of men and women throughout your organisation creates a more positive and profitable environment. Utilise the synergies that can be achieved from international, diverse groups so that you can be more innovative and successful in the longer term.

Ideas for promoting a more diverse balance in your team:
- Commit to diversity (cultural, religious, disability and gender). Be careful with your assumptions: every person and culture interprets the world and experiences in different ways. Become a 'learning leader' and ensure good cross-cultural communication and understanding in your team.
- Encourage trust-based working hours which allow people to achieve targets, but in a more flexible way.
- Encourage a 'learning culture' where people are curious and prepared for ambiguity.
- Learn to be culturally aware. You might need to adapt to deal with changes.

Personal action plan 2 Take 15 minutes to review the unit. Write down at least three important points that you have learned and that you want to apply to your change-management practice. Then commit to a schedule to implement your learning and think about how you can check if you have been successful.

	what I have learned and want to apply in my change-management practice	when/how I will apply this in my change-management practice	how I will check if I have applied it
1			
2			
3			

8 Cultural shifts

Activity file

Unit 1, Professional skills, Exercise 6

Student A
You are Donald Richardson and you will lead the communication, explaining clearly what the planned changes are, and why the company needs to implement change.

Reasons for closure
- Sales are declining in the company's western and southern European markets, so there is insufficient demand to justify this plant.
- The old plant was built in the 1930s and is now too inefficient and expensive to maintain.
- In future, the company will invest more in Latin America, where demand is increasing.
- If management doesn't take these actions, the share price will go down and the company will suffer.

Consequences
- The plant will be closed, 60% of jobs will be lost and 40% will be relocated to other UK plants. Employees can take a redundancy package or re-apply for new jobs in other locations.

Unit 2, Communication skills, Exercise 11

You are members of the management of a successful publishing house. The company publishes magazines and journals as well as books. You are debating the future of paper publications. The younger generations in your main markets are reading books and articles increasingly on electronic devices. What if you direct your investment to electronic publications and abandon paper?

Unit 2, Case study, Task 1

Management culture in the Chinese JV
- **hierarchy**: The leader in the Chinese part of the organisation plays a key role: seniority is respected, and the most senior person should be addressed first.
- **decision-making**: This is consensual (and the team needs time to discuss different proposals).
- **time**: This is cyclical and not linear, so the focus on setting objectives today for a future goal is seen differently. If the situation changes, the objectives and goals may need to change; therefore, strategic planning is not favoured, and flexibility needs to be built into planning.
- **change**: This is accepted as a natural part of life, but it's necessary to move carefully and to ensure that harmony and important elements of the old system are maintained.

Unit 3, Professional skills, Exercise 9

Suggested message
You are the director of a shipping company. One of your oil tankers has gone down in the South Pacific. You think this was caused by an explosion in the engine room which tore a hole in the side of the ship. Fortunately, the crew have all been rescued, and environmental specialists have stopped the oil from escaping. The issue now is to prevent this happening again. Therefore, the most important part of the message is that you want to urgently implement tougher mechanical safety checks for all ships. All managers should come to a meeting on April 25 from 10.00–12.00 at the company HQ to define and action the new procedures.

Unit 5, Communication skills, Exercise 8

Student A
1 You are a team leader and you have proposed to your team that you all move from private offices to an open space with other colleagues to improve communication and team work. One of your team likes working in their private office and doesn't want to move. You need to negotiate with them to gain their agreement. Your other team members have already moved to the open space and can see the advantages.
2 You are the Sales and Marketing Director of an engineering company, and one of your key products – an expensive, high-tech, eco-efficient ventilation system – just isn't selling in China, your most important new market. You believe it needs adapting so that it can be simplified and sold at a lower price. You know that the R&D team are very proud of this high-quality product, but you have to persuade the R&D Director to make the changes.

Unit 6, Professional skills, Exercise 7

Student A
You are David, a director responsible for HR. One of your 'missionaries', Henric, who has been sent to the French subsidiary, is failing to influence the local manager. The company in France is therefore experiencing increasing staff turnover and loss of talent. You have been asked to intervene. You must turn the situation around in France, but you also want Henric to stay in the job. He was put through the change-leadership development programme, as he has great potential and needed to build up more international experience and face more demanding roles in order for him to put his training into practice. You have decided that the best plan would be to give Henric some more support and one-to-one coaching, so you will focus on the following:
1 Ask Henric how things are going and what he has tried so far.
2 Explain that a key skill of a change leader is being able to influence and convince others to do things differently; try to elicit some ideas from Henric as to how he could do this.
3 Suggest that attempting to build a relationship with Michel will help, but at the same time, Henric must clearly communicate the new company direction and the priorities, and stress that supporting the new guidelines is vital for the continuing success of the company.
4 Henric should get an action plan within a week from Michel with details about what he will do and by when.
5 Henric should offer to transfer skills such as coaching and giving feedback to Michel as soon as he has his commitment.

Activity file

Unit 8, Communication skills, Exercise 9

Building a sustainability strategy

Business background

French waste company
- Company is reliant on gas as principal energy source.
- Cost of gas is increasing.
- Political problems between countries are causing a lot of disruption to pipelines.

Objective
- Need to convince stakeholders to move away from gas as its main energy supply and towards self-sufficiency.
- New strategy being implemented is to focus on producing energy from waste.
- Need to convince stakeholders that although the initial investment in technology is high, in the longer term (within ten years), this technology will reduce costs, reduce risk (dependency on external energy supply) and reduce the company's impact on the environment.

Ethos
- You have a PhD in waste management. As part of your studies, you specialised in transforming waste into energy. You have studied abroad.
- You have worked in this company a short time, but previously you worked in the largest waste company in Germany and ran international projects (Germany, US, UK, Eastern Europe). You successfully implemented an energy-from-waste project in the Czech Republic for a large automotive company and you consulted on a big project for New York City which has resulted in the NY public administration using energy from waste to power 50% of its public buildings.

Logos
- 75% of the company's factories to be self-sufficient within ten years.
- Will save the company €100m a year after ten years.
- Will create 500 jobs a year for five years for local workers (could also help gain political leverage / tax benefits).

Pathos
- You are transforming waste and reducing carbon footprint, which is good for future generations.
- It creates stability and reduces risk, thus ensuring the company's future.
- You are creating jobs for local people, thus supporting communities.
- You will invest some of the savings in better working conditions and family-friendly benefits for employees.
- The move will improve the reputation of the company and give it more moral superiority compared to rivals. This will encourage investors in the future.

Unit 1, Communication skills, Exercise 7

Student B

David: Marketing Project Manager
- You were instrumental in setting up this new team.
- You are determined to make it work, as you think the best results come from collaboration between diverse people.
- You have regular information coming in from the markets and you gather new ideas which you want to share with your team members in order to assess the viability of the ideas.

Unit 1, Professional skills, Exercise 6

Student B

You are Ivan McDonegal, an employee representative at DGO. You have been called to a meeting with some of the management team.

Read the e-mail below outlining the agenda of the meeting. Although you don't yet have all the information, you know that the plant where you and your colleagues work will be closed. This is, of course, making everybody very anxious. However, you have also recently read the company results, which show that the company is doing well globally, so you don't think the closure is justified. The plant was opened at its current location in 1936 and has been an important employer for the community since then. The closure of the plant will have a huge impact on the local community and suppliers.

> **From:** Donald Richardson
> **To:** Ivan McDonegal
> **Subject:** Urgent meeting
>
> You are asked to attend a meeting on Monday 12 September at 14.00 as a matter of priority. The management will present the following points:
> 1 Planned changes to the business
> 2 Reasons for implementing changes
> Please confirm your attendance.

Prepare some questions/arguments around the following points. You want:
- to hear what changes are planned, and why
- to clarify the justification for the closure
- to explain the impact closure will have on the local community
- information about alternatives for the workers.

During the meeting, remember to clarify information and summarise the key points.

Unit 1, Case study, Task 1

Student B

You are Peter Ledblom. A colleague, Stefano Visconti, is going to meet you to discuss the need for change.

Your position
- You are not against changes, but you think change is happening too quickly, with the consequence that quality is being lost, which you feel will cause problems in the future. You would like a minimum order-to-delivery period of seven weeks.
- You don't want to share information too widely, as you've heard that in other markets, staff turnover is high because competitors are headhunting skilled employees with the offer of more money.
- Communication is difficult due to time zones and the fact that the salespeople in other markets are often on the road and prioritise client meetings over internal communication. You feel you are often available, but not after 17:00, which is when people often try to contact you. You start early in the morning so that you can go home to your family at 17:00.
- You want to know what will happen to production in the US.

Activity file

Unit 3, Communication skills, Exercise 8

Student B
Student A is your manager. They have asked for a meeting with you. You are rather concerned because you have heard rumours that some people are going to move office and that others are going to lose their jobs. You have a good relationship with your manager – indeed, they are one of the main reasons why you enjoy your job at the moment – and you appreciate the support that they have given you, but you are worried that your boss might change and things are going to get worse rather than better for you. Get ready to express your concerns to your manager, to find out what is really going to happen and to try and get an outcome that you are happy with if possible.

Unit 3, Case study, Task 1

Student B
You are the country manager for India, based in Mumbai. You are ready to listen to what your boss has to say and to explain your plan to him. You are not very happy with the proposed changes. You have a quite informal and personal style of communication, but you tend to avoid conflict.

Unit 4, Discussion and listening, Exercise 8

Student B
You are unhappy with the changes in your department. Your manager has noticed this and phones you to talk about it.
You would like to explain to your manager that the change involved:
- some staff relocating to other units in Germany (some of your close colleagues have moved – this has demotivated you).
- a change in your role (in your previous role, you dealt with payments and invoicing on a national level; now you have been given a more responsible financial controlling role, also dealing with international subsidiaries. You are not very familiar with the tasks, so you feel insecure).
- the introduction of new processes (new business software has been introduced, but it's taking much longer that planned to roll out, and you still haven't had the training required – this is frustrating).

Unit 5, Communication skills, Exercise 8

Student B
1 You work in a private office, but your team leader and most of your team have decided they'd prefer to move to an open space with other colleagues to improve communication and team work. You find that you can focus better on your work if you have quiet surroundings, especially as you have to analyse sales contracts and figures much of the time. You don't have such a need to talk to other people; however, you like the other team members and don't want to seem unfriendly. Your team leader wants to talk to you about this issue.
2 You are the R&D Director of an engineering company, and one of your key products (manufactured in Europe) – an expensive, high-tech, eco-efficient ventilation system – just isn't selling in China, your most important new market. The Sales and Marketing Director believes it needs adapting so that it can be simplified and sold at a lower price. You're very proud of this product and you believe its success in most markets is based on its current design, so you want to find an alternative solution. One idea you have is setting up a China-specific production plant so that the same products can be produced locally at a lower cost. The Sales and Marketing Director has asked you for a meeting to discuss this.

Unit 5, Case study, Task 2

Student B
Choose one of these roles and put your point of view across to Christina.

Marcio (Quality Manager)
- You are twice Christina's age and you expect respect.
- You have worked with this team a long time; suggest that you could work with her on the implementation so that the team members see it as a joint commitment and not only coming from outside.
- Suggest you take a project-manager role, so that you could co-ordinate all the projects the team are working on.
- Stress that she would have overall responsibility for the quality system and European certification and that you would make sure everyone knew this and also how important having the European quality stamp is for the company.
- You are impressed with Christina's knowledge and professionalism, so praise her for this, but also advise her that she will have to change the way she does things, for example observe and ask more questions before telling people what to do.

Claudia (Quality Certification Senior Technician)
- Try again to organise a social event (e.g. a barbecue at the weekend at your house) and suggest you'll invite the rest of the team and their families. Stress how important it is for Christina to attend.
- Recognise any efforts Christina makes to build relationships with you.
- Explain why you have been reluctant to do the jobs (you don't respond well to being treated in what you see as a rude way, being told what to do).
- Politely give Christina some feedback on her direct communication style.
- Explain that you feel Marcio has been shut out of the project and that you all like and respect him very much and think he should have a bigger role.
- Give her some tips for working with Brazilians (to be more indirect, spend more time building relationships first, value family and local priorities).

Rodrigo (Quality Control Engineer / team leader)
- Explain that the new system is giving you lot of extra work and you have to work at weekends in order to get everything done. This is infringing on your family life, which is very important to you, so this is making you unhappy and stressed.
- Explain that the Mercosur ecological certification is vital for your Latin American business.
- Explain that you have faced many challenges in the past years from ecological organisations, local corrupt government officials, as well as indigenous groups. You have worked so hard to deal with these challenges and to negotiate solutions with them, you want to finalise this project first.

Unit 6, Communication skills, Exercise 9

Student B
You are a Ralf and you work for a food company which is internationalising. You are part of the internationalisation high-potential programme to develop future expatriate positions, to go out to other locations to spread new ideas and methods and to develop your own teams. You have a new boss, Tom, and the first goal that he has set is for you to be more open to the views of others, to resist judging ideas in order to find more creative solutions to problems and to capitalise on diversity. You have recently led a meeting, where Tom was present, about how to integrate IT systems globally. Tom has asked if you mind him giving you some feedback following the meeting. You are fine with this and pleased because:
- the meeting was very structured and although it was a challenge, you kept the team focused on the agenda and pushed the meeting along
- you made sure all the team members had a chance to speak
- you managed to stop Ramona from talking for too long about a stupid idea that you were sure wouldn't work for the Eastern European companies
- you don't know what you would do differently next time, as you felt everything went well.

Activity file

Unit 6, Professional skills, Exercise 7

Student B

You are Henric, from Sweden. You were chosen as one of the missionaries to spread the new company guidelines. You know that by now you should have at least agreed some actions with the French country manager, Michel, in order to work towards the guideline 'collective responsibility for problems, and solutions will be found together'. You have been through a company change-leadership programme and you have decided that, in this context, supporting people and giving constructive feedback should be prioritised. So far you have tried:

1 building a relationship with Michel and using a conciliatory and soft approach
2 giving Michel the feedback from the staff surveys
3 suggesting that Michel tries supporting people through coaching and giving constructive feedback to his team instead of blaming people and holding them responsible when things go wrong.

However, all your efforts so far have failed to convince Michel, and the company in France is continuing to experience increasing staff turnover and loss of talent. In fact, it's getting worse. You now feel that your training hasn't helped or that you don't have leadership qualities. You are very disappointed with yourself and you're sure you'll be taken off the job. Your manager, David, is coming over to talk to you, and you are preparing for the worst.

Unit 8, Case study, Task 2

Student B
Candidate: Stanley

Stanley comes from Hong Kong and is currently based in Kuala Lumpur. He is 45 years old and has a technical background (chemical engineering). He is married with three children. He has held positions as Technical Sales and Product Manager for two global players in the packaging industry. He has a great deal of experience in product development and of the Asian market. He has many useful contacts in the industry. He's a highly professional and well-organised manager. He's interested in this job partly because his wife has been offered a good post in the UK, so the whole family needs to relocate there. He speaks Chinese and English.

Unit 1, Communication skills, Exercise 7

Student C
Stefan: IT Team Leader

- You are responsible for all global communication systems and interfaces between logistics, suppliers and customers. Your team members are located in various locations / time zones, so it takes you time to gather information.
- Your team members are often called upon to attend to emergency technical problems to ensure the order and delivery system runs well, which is top priority for the company.
- You know you'll be under a lot of pressure in your functional role, and your wife has just had your second baby, so you are concerned about the time commitment.
- This is the first time that you have been asked to join a cross-functional team and you don't think it will be good for you professionally to say no.

Unit 3, Case study, Task 1

Student C

You are the country manager for China, based in Shanghai. You are ready to listen to what your boss has to say and to explain your plan to him. You are not very happy with the proposed changes, but you are nervous about expressing disagreement with your team leader. You have a rather indirect and non-confrontational style of communication.

Unit 6, Communication skills, Exercise 9

Student C
You are going to observe the ten-minute role-play between Student A and Student B and then give them feedback on their performance. Read their role cards on pages 61 and 93 before you start so that you understand the situation. Remember that the main purpose of feedback is to help people do better next time, so give them constructive ideas as to how they could improve their performance. In this situation, you are looking principally at how well the manager (Student A) deals with the situation, but also how successful the outcome is.

Unit 8, Case study, Task 2

Student C
Candidate: Samantha
Samantha is 31 and owns her own small business. She is originally from Singapore and moved to the UK 12 years ago. She speaks English and Malay. She started a university course in web design and marketing, but didn't complete it. Instead, she decided to travel for a year, visiting South America and the Asia-Pacific region. During her travels, she noticed how people used waste material to make new things and she was inspired by the creativity she saw. When she returned to the UK, she set up a web store selling stylish goods made in Asia. She has developed many contacts with suppliers and shippers in the region. She now wants to sell her business and run a larger operation. She doesn't have any family commitments yet.

Unit 1, Communication skills, Exercise 7

Student D
Ricardo: Sales Director
- You are always looking for new ideas for how to sell and reduce the price of your products, so you are happy to be part of the new team.
- You travel a great deal, so your only concern is that you won't be able to attend all the face-to-face meetings. But you've promised to dial in from wherever you are at the time, as you think regular communication – either face to face or on the phone – is important.
- You think the team should get together socially sometimes, to build up relationships.

Unit 3, Case study, Task 1

Student D
You are the country manager for Australia, based in Sydney. You are ready to listen to what your boss has to say. You are not very happy with the proposed changes. You have a direct style of communication and you are not afraid of confrontation.

Audio script

UNIT 1

Track 1
Gilberto: The bank had been growing by up to 20 per cent a year for many years, and its performance was still good. However, it had become such a large organisation that we could not continue managing it in the same centralised way as before. Competitors were closing the gap, and while we've always been very good at implementation, innovation and the flow of ideas within the company were not as good. I thought that we needed to change this if we were going to maintain our competitive edge.
There was some resistance. Some old-style people were saying, 'We are doing well; why should we change when we don't need to change?' It's very difficult to change a winning company, because everybody's very proud and they feel that the way they have done things for years is the right way. Some people were not able to go through this process of change, and eventually left the company. Others were mentally prepared and they wanted these changes to happen. It was hard for many mid-level executives who were used to being powerful and not having their decisions questioned. Here we were, proposing an environment where people should offer their frank opinions and where executives could no longer hide in their big offices but had to engage in open debate with their teams. There are still many people in the company who are struggling to adapt to these changes.
You have to be patient, persistent and brave at the same time. Your actions as CEO will be critical, so first of all you have to be very committed to what you are going to do. If you really are, people will follow you. The second condition is that you have to be prepared to make some tough people decisions, sometimes about colleagues. This was not an easy thing for me to do. But everybody has to understand that the company comes first; we are here to do what is best for the company.

Track 2
Serge: In my organisation, we decided to implement a change in the way we work across the globe. There were too many silos – you know, different departments and country units working in an isolated way with their own priorities – so it was difficult to work towards a common vision of collaborative, innovative thinking in order to achieve global growth.
One key problem was that people didn't share information, so we set up project teams with the aim of increasing communication across the different business units. Our aim was to encourage the sharing of new ideas and solutions to common problems. Once we'd set up the projects, I asked for comments from some managers in different areas …

Track 3
Kristina: I am based at our HQ. I am responsible for co-ordinating the budget and making the link between HQ and other business units. Sometimes I get questions from other units that I can't answer, as the top management don't want certain information to be divulged, and this can create difficulties for subsidiaries. Some people can interpret this as a lack of trust.

Track 4
Juana: In my new team, some of the members are native speakers from the US, the UK, etc., which can cause an issue. During conference calls, for example, they use expressions that we don't all understand. They also speak quickly, and our English isn't perfect, so we're too embarrassed to ask them to slow down.

Track 5
Tom: We're used to regular communication and fast response times; now, with this project structure, I often send e-mails to other members with questions, but I don't always get a response. This can be frustrating. Maybe I should call, but I don't really like the phone.

UNIT 2

Track 6
Laura: OK. Ladies and gentlemen, I'd like us to present our turnaround over the last 12 months and show you the main success factors that brought this about. Stefan, can you start by reminding us of the main problem we faced?
Stefan: Sure. Hello, everybody. Well, I'll start by setting the scene. You probably all recognise our brand of sports shoes and have seen our stores in the high street. We knew we had great products, but this wasn't enough. A year ago, we were in big trouble. Our survival was at stake because we were facing a major external threat – growing Asian competition. The main problem was that we just couldn't beat our competitors on price. I'm sure some of you have faced or are facing similar problems.
Jean-François: Excuse me, could I ask a question here?
Stefan: Of course, feel free.
Jean-François: You said that you had high prices, but how could you reduce your prices without losing quality?
Stefan: That's a good question. We decided to replace physical stores with online purchasing, which reduced our costs but still enabled us to maintain quality. However, this was just the first step. We were still just offering the products we had in stock and hoping the customer would find our site and something they liked. Sales were still too low, and this was a sign that we had another issue.

Jean-François: So what did you do?

Stefan: OK, we come to the second problem – we had ineffective marketing. We had to find a way to market and sell better than our competitors. So what did we do? We came up with a new vision where customers could create their own products – their 'dream shoes'.

Gabi: Wow, that sounds interesting! How does it work?

Stefan: The customer designs their shoe online, the order goes direct to the manufacturing plant. Then we create a customised product thanks to new computer-aided manufacturing – CAM. Finally, customer design-preference information goes straight to our marketing people for analysis. So all in all, we transformed the design and manufacturing, as well as the sales and marketing processes. Since implementation of our new plan, sales have increased by 40%.

Gabi: It sounds like you made some radical changes, but I guess some big investments in the new process as well. What was the greatest challenge?

Laura: Perhaps I can come in here. You're right – to be successful, we had to invest. We had to invest in three areas – marketing, technology and developing new skills – and we realised that we had suffered from underinvestment for some years. This involved raising finance and, with that, taking a big risk, as this would increase our exposure to debt. So I think the biggest challenge was convincing the board that in order to change and survive, we had to invest, we had to take that risk.

Track 7

Jon: Thanks to all of you for coming here today. I think we all know that although we're well known for our insulation technologies, there just aren't enough projects to guarantee future growth. We've seen reductions in all of our European markets. Governments and commercial property investors have cut back. In a way, our past success in these markets has stopped us taking risks and moving into new areas. So, we've come together to examine some alternative scenarios. Let's consider the first possibility. Laurent, can you lead on this, please?

Laurent: Sure. Well, the way I see it is this – we're a company with a good reputation and talented people, but we're weak financially and we're contracting. So, what if we merged with a larger organisation, like AKA? What would be the risks and opportunities?

Liliana: Hmm, I'm sure we'll grow. However, we'd probably lose control over the company direction.

Laurent: That's true, I agree, but AKA could offer more possibilities for us to develop professionally – you know, they are more international than we are. As we said, we know that one of our weaknesses is that we haven't moved out of our European market base. AKA is involved in big projects in the Arab Emirates and Qatar, as well as Turkey and Kazakhstan. It's well recognised for its installations, rebuilding and refurbishment. With our insulation and project-planning expertise, it would be a great partnership.

Liliana: Have you considered that they might get rid of you as soon as the merger's complete? Furthermore, our employees are likely to object – I mean, working on projects in these unfamiliar locations won't be easy. Jon, what do you think?

Jon: I can see the potential risks you've outlined, Liliana. Nevertheless, I'm certain that this merger will ensure a secure future for us. If we want to get bigger projects, it's essential that we're part of a global group, and I think we'll be an asset to them, as we have skills and specialisms that they want. In my opinion, the opportunities outweigh the risks.

Liliana: I understand your thinking, but let's examine an alternative scenario. What if …

Track 8

Fred: … so now I'd like to present to you the steps that I believe we need to take together. Firstly, we want to create a platform where all team members can exchange new ideas and ask questions across different units in order to create more innovative products. Secondly, we need to speed up decision-making by increasing delegation to individuals further down the hierarchy. Thirdly, we're going to establish a clear set of steps and deadlines for the Chinese team to follow. Finally, we aim to preserve the high quality and reliability of the products and services that customers have come to expect.

Er, Shen, you've recently graduated, haven't you? Didn't you study in the US? How would you feel about taking on some more responsibility? Can you tell us all what you think? … Are, are there any comments? Can we have a show of hands? Who's in favour?

UNIT 3

Track 9

Adriano: In Brazil, we're used to things changing. At work, it seems like there's always something new happening. I think some of our managers are influenced by their education abroad, so they talk about a lot of theories. In reality, though, when our managers told us our department was being restructured, we had meetings to talk about our ideas, but those ideas didn't go up very far. The senior managers are still quite powerful and they'd already decided what was going to happen – we didn't really take part in the process. In the end, the change was used as a way of getting rid of people, but they didn't want to tell us that. So now when I hear 'change', I worry. For me – and I think for my team – the most important thing is to have trust and respect from our bosses. If something is going to change, and we have a grievance, we want to know that we can speak openly and not suffer consequences. I don't have to be a part of every change decision, but if I don't like something, I want to be listened to. Most of all, we want our boss to be honest about what's going to happen. We don't really feel this was the case the last time.

Track 10

Sanjay: We're a growing entrepreneurial company, based in India. A lot of the engineers are young, like myself. We have a lot of energy and ideas and we feel we can drive the company forward. Things are changing fast. Our boss is much older than many of us, and he's kind of like our guide and mentor. On the one hand, he listens to us and on the other hand, he sets the limits, so we can't take too many big risks, but we are free to experiment within those limits. At the same time, we depend totally on him, as he's like the eyes and ears of the organisation, always looking for threats and opportunities. Recently, our boss saw a problem was coming, so he invited us to a meeting and presented the situation. Then he said, 'Tell me, what shall we do about it?' Together, we came up with solutions and agreed what we could change and what we wanted to keep – like our healthcare, for example. We rely on our healthcare and other insurance benefits: this is very important for us and our families, and even when other things change, the company is careful to preserve these key things. I think you can say that we're engaged, as we feel we're in partnership with the organisation, so we don't fear change. We feel like our boss is our friend, and the company helps us and our families. It's important that we have a harmonious relationship with our employer.

Track 11

Erika: I've worked for this company for 15 years and I think I've seen maybe three or four change programmes in that time, sometimes instigated by senior managers, and during our merger with the Swedish company, a change consultancy was brought in initially. You could say I'm a bit sceptical about some of those past change initiatives, as they didn't really involve us enough, and as a consequence, the results were not that positive. We've had so many problems post-merger, so now a new CEO's been brought in, a Swedish woman. She's taken a really different approach, and I have to say it's refreshing. She asked each department to look at the company vision and come up with a list of things we were doing well already and a list of things that could be done better to achieve the company goals. She looked at our lists and said, 'OK, make sure your people know what they're doing well and ask them what steps they'll take in the areas that need improving, and report back to me in six months.' As a result, our team feels good about the things we're doing well and we feel even better about the fact that we can decide what to change and how to do it. We know our area and our people better than anybody, and we feel this has been recognised. We like the fact that nobody's telling us what to do, no external consultants are interfering with their latest theory. We just feel we've been trusted to make the changes we feel are necessary in the way we think best. I haven't felt this engaged in all the years I've worked for this company.

Track 12

Albert: This is a great company, and our loyal workforce has been the key to our success up to now. However, our current offer doesn't have a future. I'd like to hear your views on what we can do to change. So the question is, where should we be going in the next three years?

Yoko: The business is in big trouble. The sooner we communicate this, the better. I'd like to call a meeting of staff within the month and report that we have a problem.

Albert: Thanks, Yoko. I agree that it's important to be open and honest with staff, but we also need a plan going forward. What can we do to change and survive?

Gail: Can't we retrain people for different jobs? If we can offer people alternative work, this'll show that we care about them. We should set up a virtual service where staff work from home. Most of the photos that people take are not great quality, especially from mobile phones. We could offer a service, using specialist software that most people can't afford, to improve photos.

Param: I agree with Gail – the Internet is the future, and we need a positive message. We could also use selected photos to produce professional videos with music, albums, T-shirts. Not everyone has the time or expertise to do this kind of thing. Let's ask staff if they like these ideas or if they have any other thoughts.

Albert: Thanks, everybody, that's great. Erm, let's summarise and agree what we're going to communicate. So, you're saying that although we'll need to close stores, people can be home-based, they'd just need some training in the new software which we can install on a virtual network. I think we need to stress that although this means a big change in the way we work, jobs would be safe. I think that's a good message.

I'll leave you now to follow up on actions, and we'll meet again on May the 15th to make sure we have all the information in place prior to the staff meeting. Thanks for your contributions, you're a great team.

Track 13

Yoko: I'm sorry to sound negative, but really, Param, how will asking staff for ideas and suggesting different ways to work actually resolve our financial difficulties?

Param: Yoko, it's our job to motivate people, support them and set clear guidelines and goals. If we do this, I'm sure we will get the results we need. I'll produce a proposal for the May 15th meeting.

Gail: And I'll outline the services we can offer with budget and technical requirements. Yoko, can I work with you on the financial aspects?

Yoko: OK, yes, let's meet on Tuesday morning. But my biggest concern is that whilst we're talking and asking and retraining and all that, we'll run out of money. Personally, I think we have to do something much more radical and fast. We need to be clear and tell staff that unless we cut stores and jobs first, we won't be in a position to restructure, but then no one listens to me …

UNIT 4

Track 14

Talal: The first job is to identify the 'influencers' in the organisation, the key people who need to be brought into the process somehow. One such person was Marco, who had a powerful position with a lot of benefits and autonomy – you know, he was in a good place. So, what happened? In the rationalisation process, many of his superiors took a generous exit package and left. I'm sure he feared losing power, especially as the senior team had changed, but in fact, he still had a lot of influence over the whole department. He was very loyal, and the way he represented his people's position meant that they all stood behind him. I felt that the new management couldn't afford to lose his backing. So what did we do? We asked Marco what we could exchange for his support and we discovered that a key bargaining point was to assure him that his team would be protected. It's always advisable to listen to influential people and negotiate with them if you can. In this way, you get their support and the support of others.

Track 15

Talal: Now I'd like to tell you about Helmut. He was quite young, he was climbing the career ladder and he'd formed good relations with his boss in middle management, who supported him and pushed his career along. During the merger, much of middle management was taken out, so he lost his sponsor and found himself without relationships. He was also very angry that so many people had been made redundant. Helmut became increasingly opposed to the changes. Initially, some people agreed with him, but in time, most of the team adapted to the changes and got on with the job to be done. Helmut became more isolated in his negative attitude, so we took the following steps. We started by having a series of one-to-one discussions, to listen to his grievances and to look for ways to help him adapt. Next, we established objectives to improve his attitude and behaviour. All employees are given time to work through their anger and frustration, but there comes a point where people have to move on to the next phase – acceptance. If they can't do that, then in the end, you go to the last phase: you tell them to go. Unfortunately, that's what happened to Helmut.

Track 16

Rui: Hello, Rui Silveira speaking.
Jean: Hello, Rui, it's Jean. How are things going?
Rui: Well, I'm OK, but things aren't easy at the moment.
Jean: Well, as I said in my e-mail, the reason I'm calling you today is to start helping you through the issues that you told me about. If I can recap, you said that you're not happy with the organisational changes and the new process that we've introduced. This will be the first of several calls, but today, can you prioritise what you see as the main problem?
Rui: Well, there are a lot of things. I've lost some good colleagues, including my boss. I'm not really sure what I should be doing any more. I just feel a lot of pressure and I'm …
Jean: I'm sorry, Rui, could I just interrupt you for a moment?
Rui: Yes, of course.
Jean: I know that right now it seems like everything is too much, as you said. So let's try to break this problem into small steps. What exactly is stopping you from doing your job well?
Rui: Well … before when I went into work, I knew exactly what I had to do, how to do it and who I was reporting to. Now I'm confused about all this.
Jean: Right, so what you're saying is you're not clear about your role? Shall we focus on that today?
Rui: That would be good, yes.

Track 17

Jean: OK, Rui. What have you done so far to establish your role and responsibilities?
Rui: Last month, we had that conference call with you and all the team, and I asked what I should be doing. Um, you said I needed to connect to the new system, then plan actions to achieve the overall goals you'd set and report back.
Jean: So, did you do that?
Rui: No, because I haven't had enough time to transfer all the data across. But more important is that I'm not sure how my role fits with what the others are doing, so I can't set my goals. I'm accustomed to more, you know, direction.
Jean: How could you clarify what you and others should be doing?
Rui: I suppose I could talk more to my new team leader, Mr Schmidt, get some help to integrate my system, then ask him if we can have a team meeting to establish, er, who's doing what, agree some targets … This will help, but I don't know him very well.
Jean: That sounds like a really good idea. What do you need to do to arrange that meeting?
Rui: Well, I could talk to Mr Schmidt on Monday and, if he agrees, ask him to send round an e-mail to arrange the meeting.
Jean: When you have the meeting, what could stop you from achieving your goals?
Rui: We're a new team. We don't all know each other that well – maybe the communication will be difficult. We really need someone to guide us a bit, help us to clarify our roles.
Jean: Do you think Mr Schmidt can do that?
Rui: Yes, I guess so. He is the leader.
Jean: I think you'll find Mr Schmidt very supportive once he understands the issues. OK, so could you just go through what we've talked about? What are you going to do, by when and how will you know if you've been successful?
Rui: On Monday, I'll talk to Mr Schmidt and ask him to arrange a meeting with our team. Then, with his help, we'll look at the objectives and decide who is going to do what, by when. If we manage to achieve that, I'll feel we've made progress.
Jean: That's great – and I'd like you to know that I do understand your position. Here at FW Net, we're used to running very autonomous teams. You've come from a different culture at Bamberg and, as you said, you're used to more direction. But don't worry, we're here to support you.

Audio script

Track 18

Guillaume: The team doesn't seem to work, as we have many new members and we don't know each other very well. It's difficult when the leader is so busy. We suggested to you that we should all go out for a meal or something to get to know each other better, but you always seem too busy, so this still hasn't happened.

Ben: I'm very busy with planning at the moment and I have a lot of conference calls with senior management, so I don't have much time for socialising. We have a big job to do. I expect my team to be autonomous. I've set the targets and it's up to you to find a way to achieve them.

Ellen: But we're not very clear about what we should be doing. We have this target to cut our budget by 20%, but we don't know *what* we should cut or *how*. We didn't use to work like this. Some people think we need the best modern offices in a prime central location, you know, for prestige, to impress clients, so we can't just move to cheaper offices. Others don't want to lose their company cars or travel allowances; others like the staff restaurant. We're a team. Who has the authority to decide what we cut in the end?

Ben: That's why I want to reward the team member who achieves the most savings, as motivation.

Guillaume: What do you mean – a bonus for the person who achieves most savings? We're supposed to be working together here – what is this individual bonus about? Are we supposed to compete with each other? This is really bad for morale.

Ben: I think you all have to realise that things can't be relaxed and friendly all the time. Declaire Engineering was inefficient – that's why it's been taken over.
I think the reward system will encourage people to be more ambitious, so it'll help to change the company culture for the better.

UNIT 5

Track 19

Interviewer: Farida, how do you identify the key people in your company who have the potential to spread change?

Farida: When I want people to change the way they do something, first I try to convince those who are naturally good salespeople, those who are well connected within informal or formal networks in the company.

Interviewer: Can you give us some examples of these networks?

Farida: Well, we have more formal arrangements, like cross-functional project groups for example. Through these groups, you can introduce changes. But networks can also be the groups that go out together socially, after work. In our company, we identified one group of employees from different departments that trained together as a triathlon team and competed every year. This wasn't something formally organised, and the members of the team ranged from senior managers to workers on the factory floor. They told me, 'In this team, we are equal. We have no hierarchy and we have become good friends.'

Track 20

Interviewer: Farida, once you've identified a network in your organisation, what's the next step?

Farida: We look for the members of this group who are the organisers, the ones that 'connect' people and make things happen. Principally, these people tend to be very good at building rapport. If you can get these people on board, they have the potential to influence others.

Interviewer: You mentioned that these people tend to be 'very good at building rapport'. What exactly do you mean?

Farida: When I say 'building rapport', I mean that they make an effort to get to know new people, they listen and take an interest in them, and they try to see the world through the eyes of others.

Interviewer: And how can you successfully spread change through these people? How can they influence others?

Farida: You'll find that people in the group or network with a wide range of good relationships are listened to. So you can start with this, and then you can build other skills with training and coaching.

Interviewer: What other skills do you try to develop?

Farida: I'd say they need to be able to communicate with different people and at different times, in different ways. Sometimes they need to listen and support, and sometimes it's necessary to give a strong, clear message and to focus on goals. They also need to identify who needs to be brought on board to make things work. They also need to deal with any people who are 'blocking' the achievement of goals.

Track 21

Thomas: I travel a lot, as I like to meet people face to face, and we keep in touch through our personal Facebook accounts. I also put people in touch with other useful contacts – this helps the team work better, especially when we're all over the world.
I try to increase my visibility and improve connections between people. I do this by arranging social activities and sports teams at my factory and I organise an annual international meeting. This is a great opportunity to bring different groups together.
I'm told that I help the global teams because I try to see their position, by listening to them and asking questions. Then I make management aware of their situation. I also facilitate communication in virtual meetings between HQ and the subsidiaries, especially if some people don't speak English so well.
Because I build positive relationships and encourage networking in the company, senior managers often ask me to help persuade people to accept change.

Track 22

Al: Hello, I'm Al. It's Consuela, isn't it? Nice to meet you face to face at last! Would you like a coffee?'

Consuela: Hello, Al. Yes, it's nice to put a face to the voice on the phone! Coffee sounds good, espresso if you have it.

Al: So, er, how are things going for you?

Consuela: Well, I'm managing the plant now, so I'm really pleased. In fact, do you remember Jack Nuñez, the Operational Director? You put me in touch with him a while ago. He's the one who sponsored me, he really helped me get the job, so he was a fantastic contact. I've got you to thank for that!

Al: Congratulations! I'm glad Jack could help. That's what we should be doing in the company – helping each other, don't you agree? One espresso – there you are. Well, it's good of you to come over today.

Track 23

Al: I won't take too much of your time, Consuela, but we need to talk about the start date for implementing the new SCM software system. I think you know why we're doing this. The car-parts supply business is getting tougher – we need to be faster and offer a more efficient service. We can do this by integrating our production better with our customers and suppliers. But, firstly, I'd like to hear *your* views and find out how *you* feel about this.

Consuela: I'm sure you're right that we need to get this new software, Al. But you know we'll have a lot of extra costs this year, and our budget is already really stretched.

Al: Hm. What extra costs exactly will you incur?

Consuela: Well, we'll have to re-allocate people to this project and we'll have to pay consultants to come in. Our network is older, so it'll need a lot more upgrading to be compatible with this new system. This could take until the end of the year. That's a lot of time and resources.

Al: I hear what you're saying. You're concerned about the cost and time pressures this'll add to your part of the business. Have you considered the benefits you'll get?

Consuela: Well, I guess after a year or so, we'll see some benefits.

Al: Can I ask you what your priorities are over the next couple of years?

Consuela: My main priority is to reduce the order errors and returns. Our target is to cut this by at least 20% over the next two years.

Al: I see. Well, I think you'll find the new system will ensure you achieve that target and more.

Consuela: Do you think so? Yes, I suppose it could …

Track 24

Al: So, can I summarise the key points? We need the software to be installed this year in order to increase our competitive edge, but you feel you don't have the budget. However, you think that the new system will help you to achieve your targets. Can we agree, then, that the sooner we implement the new system, the better it is for both of us?

Consuela: Yes, that's right.

Al: We're working towards the same goal here, so let's see what we can do with the budget. Do you have some money you could re-allocate from lower priority areas?

Consuela: I suppose we have the facilities budget – you know, for the offices, new furniture and so on. We also have a discretionary budget for staff bonuses, but …

Al: OK, so why don't we divert the facilities budget to this project and link staff bonuses to achievement of the implementation goals? We can keep the use of consultants to a minimum and, to save more costs, I can second one of my people to your team for, say, six months. How does that sound?

Consuela: Mm, I don't know … I guess we could do that.

Al: Great! So, we have an agreement. Can you draw up a schedule? I'll get things moving from my end.

Track 25

Eric Huang: Firstly, you need to successfully build relationships with a diverse range of people in a variety of contexts. Create opportunities to meet people, use the phone rather than e-mail. Choose behaviour that's comfortable for your international counterparts. Do they usually maintain eye contact or avoid it? Do they tend to stand close to you or further away? Listen and ask follow-up questions about the subjects that your partner talks about. Find out what's important to them and take interest in these things. In summary, you should meet the other person's expectations. All of this is very important to build the trust which underlies all relationships.

Next, it's important to think about your communication style. It's really important to develop flexibility. In some cultures, like Scandinavian ones for example, people often appreciate more direct communication and feedback, while in others, like Latin American or Asian ones, people may find this uncomfortable or even offensive. So in those cases, you'll need to be more indirect. There are some situations when you should present a clear, strong message and other times when it's better to just listen and ask questions.

Finally, it's useful to recognise where political power lies in organisations and understand how best to use this to achieve objectives. In some cultures, like in China, it's very important to respect hierarchy, and you must influence the leader first. In others, like the US, it may be someone lower down the organisational structure who is influential, because they have a strong network of contacts or specialised knowledge. And it's equally important to think about the people who influence the influencers. It's a bit like a political leader and their people – you often have to convince the majority first. This is especially true when you're trying to change things.

Track 26

Marcio: I'm twice her age and have worked with this team a long time. I'm very impressed by Christina's knowledge and her professionalism, but she wants to do things her way. I could advise her and help to get the team on board, if she asked me.

Track 27

Claudia: Well, she's been here three months, and I don't think she's been out with us once, not even for a drink. She just works all the time, so we haven't had a chance to get to know her. And I know she doesn't mean it, but she can come across as quite direct, even rude, so I don't always do the task that she's given me.

Track 28

Rodrigo: I don't have a problem with Christina, but this new system is giving me a lot of extra work. She hasn't asked what other jobs my team has this year, like the Mercosur ecological certification, which is so vital for us. We've been working really hard to achieve that.

UNIT 6

Track 29

Interviewer: Ana, what skills have you found are necessary for managing change?

Ana: It's hard to say which skills are more important, but what I have found the most vital and, actually, really hard to develop, are skills which enable you to 'sell' the change across the organisation. This means getting to know the right people and then adapting your message and approach. So for me, we need to learn how to develop the rapport-building skills to establish and maintain appropriate relationships within and outside the organisation; and presentation skills focusing on adapting key messages to your audience.

Interviewer: You said that these skills are difficult to develop ... so how did you go about it?

Ana: Well, I wanted to improve my presentation skills, so, through interpersonal and intercultural training, I focused on learning to be more empathetic. That means trying to see things from other people's and other culture's perspectives. Then I could adapt my messages and the style of presentation to better fit my audience. In fact, I learned something else really important from this. By learning to look at things differently, this also helped me become more creative and innovative when I was looking for solutions. This is so vital for leading change.

Track 30

Interviewer: François, what skills are important to have as a change leader, and how do you get those skills?

François: In my case, we had to deal with the closure of one of our three plants. In this kind of change, it's very important to consider carefully which people you will need in the new structure, how existing jobs will change, and which positions will become obsolete. Unfortunately, this often means that, as a manager, you will have to learn how to have those difficult conversations with people, as well as the motivational ones. In my experience, as long as people are clear about their position, what they need to do and how they fit into the new structure or not, it's possible for people to move forward. So the key skills to develop for me are: how to coach and mentor those who will have to leave, and to help them to plan alternatives for the future. Then you have to define and delegate the remaining roles and responsibilities clearly and motivate these people, so that they get on with the business of rebuilding the company for the future. To help me do this, I took part in a leadership development programme with a specific emphasis on coaching and motivation.

Interviewer: How do you develop motivational skills?

François: First, you learn to identify what motivates different people. That could be money, but often it's positive relationships with the team or senior management, or having plenty of autonomy, for example. Then I had training in giving and receiving feedback as a way of motivating and improving performance. This is really difficult to do well, but I think it's a very important skill for a manager to learn.

Interviewer: So do you feel that, with the right training, leaders can develop skills to cope with even the most difficult aspects of change management?

François: Many necessary skills can be developed, as I've mentioned. However, there are others that personally I think can't be. You have to be very resilient and you have to have confidence in yourself and in what you are doing, as you'll almost certainly be unpopular and be criticised by many people.

Track 31

Bill: Can we review progress so far?

Karin: Of course.

Bill: Can you tell me how you think things are going?

Karin: Well, this was a new and tough job for me. We had to find ways to streamline all of the processes and improve the productivity of the team in order to return the unit to profit, and all in six months! So yes, I'm pleased with progress. I met the targets.

Bill: Yes, I can see that. I've noticed that you've been working very hard to build a motivated team, and we've seen some interesting new ideas coming from your people. This means that people are starting to change the way they do things. By encouraging a really innovative approach, business performance is definitely improving.

Karin: That's good to hear, thank you.

Bill: I think it's also important that we learn something from each experience. So can we talk about what needs to be improved? Is there anything you think you could have done better?

Karin: Well, we've lost a couple of really good people who I wanted in the team. They weren't happy with a couple of decisions I made or how I acted. That was disappointing, and to be honest, it's caused me some stress, you know ... It's not always easy.

Bill: In the end, some people will always be unhappy, but do you think you could have given them more of your time? You know, perhaps listened to their concerns a bit more? I've noticed that you're very focused on the goals, which is great, but I'd like to see you focus more on the people, too.

Track 32

Bill: So, now that we've reviewed some outcomes of the project, on reflection, what would you do differently next time?

Karin: Well, I'm not sure. I mean, I was given the targets, and to achieve them, some people had to go. I'm not sure that I could have changed that.

Bill: Well, perhaps if you'd spent more time supporting those who had to leave, do you think it could have helped?

Karin: The outcome would have been the same, but I suppose I could have done more to help those people move on.

Bill: I'm also concerned about you. How could I help you more? You're very independent and you never ask for help. I think you'd benefit from sharing some of the load with me or asking your team for more support. I'm sure your people would react positively. It's important for a leader to show they're human sometimes, you know ... Considering this, what kind of support do you think would help you in future?

Karin: Hm, well, maybe something to help me understand people better – that might help. Especially as this is a different working style for me, you know – different to back home.

Bill: Yes, I recognise that the way things work here, the way we communicate, may be different to what you're used to.

Karin: And if you want me to spend more time with people and share more stuff, maybe you could give me more space to achieve the goals, a bit more flexibility?

Bill: OK, so let's summarise the action points. To help you on the people side, we'll look at some coaching and mentoring development, some training in adapting your working style. And I'll think about how we can support you more, build in some flexibility … How does that sound?

Track 33

Pamela: Hi, Jean-Claude. Are you OK?

Jean-Claude: Not really. It's Petra again.

Pamela: Oh, what's happened?

Jean-Claude: It's Ken Wang – you know, my sales guy for Asia. Petra was criticising his work in front of everyone in the meeting, because a customer had complained about the way Ken dealt with a problem.

Pamela: I'm sure she didn't mean to offend him. Petra just has a very strong focus on our customers, because this is such an important part of the improvement process we've introduced. Remember, 'always prioritise the customer's needs' and all that. She's just trying to help the team improve our service, so we can achieve our goal.

Jean-Claude: I think it's good for us to be more customer-focused, but you know, it's hard sometimes if we get it wrong. The comments are always so negative, and I don't think this kind of feedback should be given to someone in front of the others.

Pamela: Well, you see it as negative. I think for her, it's constructive. I think the real problem is that there are very different expectations of what feedback means in the team.

Jean-Claude: You could be right, but you know, for Ken to lose face like that is really serious for him. He's really valuable for our team, he has excellent technical knowledge. We don't want to demotivate him and we certainly don't want to lose him. I don't think Petra has thought about the impact of her style on different people. She doesn't seem to be very aware.

Pamela: Hmm, I see what you mean.

Jean-Claude: Shall I raise this at the next team meeting? It would be good to discuss expectations about feedback and how we give it.

Pamela: Yes, why not? Let's discuss it and get some agreement on what kind of feedback we want and how it's delivered. I think Petra will be open to that.

UNIT 7

Track 34

Interviewer: Hakon, how did you go about setting goals?

Hakon: The hardest part is defining what success is going to mean, as it can mean different things to different people. So you need a wide range of SMART objectives.

Interviewer: What do you mean by 'SMART objectives'?

Hakon: Objectives need to be specific, measureable, achievable, relevant and time-bound … that means set within defined time limits.

Interviewer: I see. So once you'd defined how you'd set the objectives, what was the next step?

Hakon: Well, the first question we asked is, 'Who has a say in deciding on the measures of success?'. It's very important to invite a broad base of stakeholders to help you define the goals.

Interviewer: So was it important for you to bring in people from the new organisation?

Hakon: Oh yes, this was essential. We'd come into a new company in a different part of the world whose employees didn't know us and were therefore quite suspicious of us. When measurement is the job of a small group, everyone else ends up feeling judged. And when people are judged, they tend to get defensive – they hide mistakes and often blame others. It's better if everyone can take credit for successes and responsibility for fixing mistakes.

Interviewer: So, once you'd established who was going to set the goals, how did you decide which goals to prioritise?

Hakon: Once we'd formed a representative group, we agreed the most important goals. These are often legal requirements, that sort of thing. Firstly, we had to introduce rules for compliance, in order to bring the new business into line with our existing operations and EU rules. So the first step was to ensure strict adherence to regulations for managing the forestry, more protection of workers' rights and so on.

Interviewer: And are some goals easier to measure than others?

Hakon: When you're talking about making sure people follow technical procedures, targets are easier to define. Other key things like a commitment to sustainability and ethical behaviour, for example, are more difficult to measure, but we had to find ways to do it.

Track 35

Interviewer: So, Hakon, what did you measure exactly?

Hakon: There are four kinds of results you can measure: behaviour you can see, feedback you can hear, experiences you can feel and numbers you can count. If you cover these four areas, then you'll get a comprehensive list of data that people can relate to and aim to achieve every day. So we took these four areas and measured things like: Were new health-and-safety checks signed off each week? Were the records filled in correctly? How many issues were reported, and were they dealt with adequately? Did people understand the sustainability agenda, and was there evidence of actions taken to contribute to this agenda?

Did people feel happy doing the tasks? What were the frustrations? Did they have enough time? And so on.

Interviewer: And what was the most difficult thing to measure?

Hakon: The most difficult aspect was probably measuring levels of ethical behaviour. This is partly because the expectations of local communities, environmental groups, local politicians and others can sometimes conflict with the goals of an international company like ours. Local managers told us that in order to get agreement with all these parties and avoid bad publicity, they can't always follow our guidelines as exactly as we normally try to. So I say, when you face a moral challenge like this, you have to understand the complexities of the local situation.

Interviewer: What advice would you have for others facing a situation like this?

Hakon: Listen to local managers and don't be too quick to judge. Sometimes we measure too much, based on our own experience. In unfamiliar contexts, it's important to build more flexibility into your targets.

Interviewer: And did you achieve your goals? Was the change successful?

Hakon: Well, change is an ongoing process, and in some areas we've succeeded and in others we've fallen short. The main thing is to track progress and make corrections as needed, learning what's worked and what hasn't. The first objective of measuring change is to learn, and I repeat this every day: we learn from success and we learn even more from failure. I can't emphasise enough how important this is. If people are afraid to make a mistake, the change will fail. In this case, mistakes have been made and problems have occurred, but we've turned this into learning for all.

Track 36

Saheed: When you're implementing change, it's very important to be clear about what you're doing, how you'll do it, why, and finally, how you evaluate the whole process. One way to do this is by using SMART objectives. Let's look at this ... The 'S' stands for 'specific' – this means the goal is clear and unambiguous. To make goals specific, they must tell a team exactly what's expected, why it's important, who's involved, and where it's going to happen. Ask yourself these questions: How will you know if you're successful? What does success mean in relation to this project or goal? What does success mean to different people? How do you measure both positive and negative impacts of change?

Secondly, 'M' is for 'measurable'. Measuring progress is supposed to help a team stay on track, reach its target dates and experience the sense of achievement that motivates it to put in the continued effort required to reach the ultimate goal. So decide clearly: What can you measure?

Next, we move onto 'A', which is 'achievable'. This stresses the importance of goals that are realistic and attainable. You should be able to develop the attitudes, skills and financial capacity to reach them. So consider the following questions: Are the goals realistic? Have you considered all the possible obstacles?

Now we'll look at what I consider to be the most important of all – 'relevant'. This stresses the importance of choosing goals that matter. Many times, you'll need support to accomplish a goal: resources, a champion, someone to remove obstacles ... Are your goals relevant to your boss, your team, your organisation? Will you receive that necessary support? And finally, the 'T' is for 'time-bound'. It's key to set goals within a time frame, giving them a target date. A commitment to a deadline helps a team focus its efforts on completion of the goal on or before the due date. This part of the SMART goal criteria is intended to prevent goals from being overtaken by the day-to-day crises that invariably arise in an organisation. A time-bound goal is intended to establish a sense of urgency, often essential in change initiatives. So ask yourself – what milestones and deadlines will you set?

Track 37

Susan: Susan Krabbe speaking.

Ron: Susan, it's Ron.

Susan: Hi, Ron. How are you doing?

Ron: Not good, Susan. Did you see the e-mail from Fabio that I forwarded to you? Unbelievable! You know, it's all about control. They don't trust us. That's the main thing – it's the lack of trust.

Susan: Ron, I ...

Ron: And how do they expect us to do all this new fancy project management? Nobody here is trained to do this – it's just not possible or practical to use sophisticated tools like this. It's logistically impossible.

Susan: Ron, calm down. This isn't about trust. Fabio's right. The way we manage projects in this company is a mess. We need to change things. I know it feels like we're losing control, but it's not that, I don't think. It's just about change – creating a new system and managing the change with new reporting.

Ron: But the ideas really don't make sense. We're losing flexibility, we're giving up control of key projects which affect our business here, and, you know, the amount of work all this generates, reporting back to Boston, and for what benefit? And these 'metrics' – budget and time. They're important, but too mechanical – it'll stop people thinking about quality, which is the most important thing. I'm going to have to fight these proposals. We need to keep our independence so we can run the right projects here in the right way – our way!

UNIT 8

Track 38

Etsuko: We started this change process over 12 years ago – in fact, it was more like a gradual process of transformation. In our case, the company needed more creativity and new ideas in order to maintain its position, and we've been through many steps to get to where we are now.

Interviewer: So how did the company start the process?

Etsuko: A new CEO was brought in, and he took the company international, but there were many conflicts in those early years. He just couldn't change the way people thought as quickly as he wanted to. For example, it was almost impossible to change the attitudes and practices of some of the existing ageing, conservative, white male management team, and this was a real obstacle.

Interviewer: So what did he do?

Etsuko: Well, as these people progressively retired, instead of replacing them with similar managers already working in the company, he started to bring new people into key positions, like me, and as you can see, I'm a woman and I am from Japan, so I have a different perspective.

Interviewer: And what was your mission?

Etsuko: My main task was to devise a global HR strategy to develop more diverse and creative teams. This means that, at all levels, we want our employees to contribute different perspectives. They must be ready to take risks and they should always be looking for learning opportunities. Finally, they must be continually rethinking the needs of the business.

Track 39

Interviewer: So how did you go about doing this?

Etsuko: We started by setting goals for diversity and creativity at work, and measurements were put in place to check progress. Over time, we set up family-friendly policies to enable women with children to balance tough jobs with family commitments, and we put in place employee-rotation schemes. Managers were asked to give employees more autonomy, and we introduced a company-wide training programme bringing people together from all global locations to work on new ideas. And what's really essential, all of this was backed up by compatible policies for reward and promotion.

Interviewer: So was this change easy to achieve?

Etsuko: No, it certainly wasn't! It's taken many years and much determination to get to this point. Although I had the support of our CEO, others at the top never really accepted or supported me. I started to make real progress about five years ago, when the people who were blocking me were finally replaced and so the culture started to change.

Interviewer: So what's your advice for others in a similar position?

Etsuko: I know others in my position who have given up, but you have to be resilient, patient and very persistent. More importantly, you have to get that message to the employees. You know, they can become very disillusioned if you start talking about change but they don't see it happening.

Interviewer: How did you eventually get change established?

Etsuko: Firstly, there are no short cuts – you have to go through all the steps to get there, so you may only see new things happening many years down the line. Secondly, eventually all the people involved need to see positive results. If not, that change will not last.

Interviewer: And now, what is the new culture like?

Etsuko: We have a new mission statement: 'Diversity and creativity is key, and we are ready to address change.' Leaders must inspire and support this or they will become irrelevant.

Track 40

Section 1

Dr Takamoto: Good afternoon, my name is Dr Roberto Takamoto and I work for the United Nations Environment Programme. Before that, I was a senior executive in Unilever and was responsible for the successful implementation of large-scale sustainability practices which increased sales and brand value. In addition, I have worked in Brazil, the USA and Japan and have also been a visiting lecturer at major international universities.

Track 41

Section 2

Dr Takamoto: I'd like to start by presenting to you the scenario. We're facing three key challenges: population growth, increasing global demand for environmental resources, and environmental stress due to climate change. Population growth, increasing demand on resources and climate change. These three factors combined mean we're facing a completely unsustainable future, unless we change our business culture.

Between 2010 and 2030, demand is projected to grow by 33% for primary energy, 80% for steel, 27% for cereals and 41% for water. How can we meet this demand and guarantee sustainability? There is a win–win solution. Although some are still focused on short-term gain, many companies see longer-term sustainability as a key driver of innovation and change. Sustainability has created new opportunities, and consumer demand for sustainable products is growing. For example, GE saw sales of its Ecomagination products reach 18 billion dollars in 2009, with the company predicting revenue growth for these products at twice the rate of the total revenues in a few years. So, you see, it really makes business sense to invest in sustainability.

Track 42

Section 3

Dr Takamoto: If we don't change now, our fertile and flowing economies and planet will become dry like a desert. You are the leaders of our global businesses today. Ask yourself this: 'How can I ensure the future success of my company, and what legacy will I leave for the next generations?' I think you'll find the answer lies in encouraging radical thinking and fomenting innovation and change, to create solutions that are both profitable and sustainable. In a world of shrinking opportunities, sustainability is the great untapped well just waiting to explode.

Track 43

Speaker 1

Marc: Ravi had an interesting proposal at the meeting, and I was really asking him a lot of questions – you know, trying to challenge his thinking, but in a creative way. I think we have to examine all the pros and cons, don't we? Since then, Ravi has been very quiet. I'm afraid I've upset him, but I'm not sure why …

Track 44
Speaker 2

Susanna: I felt there wasn't much structure to the meeting, and we seemed to spend a lot of time talking. It wasn't clear to me what the agenda was or the real purpose of this meeting. I'm very busy and I was a little frustrated that the meeting went on for so long. I think we should have all submitted our proposals in advance, and these could have been examined and recommendations made by a smaller group. This is how we do it at home, and I think it is a more efficient way to do things.

Track 45
Speaker 3

Ravi: We thought it was a very interesting meeting ... Yes, we like to listen to all the different ideas – there's no problem – but I wasn't sure it was the right place to discuss some of the issues ... Marc seemed determined to talk about the problems we've been having with the new extraction technique ...

Track 46
Speaker 4

Crystal: Well, I thought it was fantastic, very interesting. It's true there was a lot of discussion, but this brought out some great ideas and some really creative conflict as well. This is necessary if we're going to really get new ideas. The only thing I noticed was that Susanna seemed really impatient – you know, she didn't really want to listen to all the ideas. She didn't seem to get the purpose of the meeting at all – she was in such a hurry to finish. Maybe we should have made it clear beforehand what everybody expected to get out of the meeting – or maybe have another meeting to discuss the specific problems that were identified – I don't know, really.

Answer key

1 Change happens

A 2 *Suggested answers*: Change happens when an organisation:
becomes too large/ reacts to a downturn in the business / innovates / responds to markets or clients / responds to shifts in lifestyle / exists in a highly competitive environment / believes in continuous improvement / merges with another organisation / demerges / experiences a change in management / relocates / expands / grows / globalises / downsizes / increases mechanisation or technology / reacts to extreme circumstances such as a natural disaster, terrorist attack or war / faces political shifts / faces alterations in government policy or funding / listens to employees' ideas.

3 The quote is based on the saying 'If it ain't broke, don't fix it' and means that you should always be looking for improvements in your business/service/product. Some companies implement a continuous improvement programme similar to the Japanese idea of *kaizen*. Others focus on continuous innovating.

4 a Organisation was too large and complex, couldn't manage in same centralised way.
Competitors were closing the gap.
Innovation and flow of ideas were not as good as they should be.
b To maintain their competitive edge
c It was a winning company.
d It was hard for many mid-level executives, who were used to being powerful and not having their decisions questioned. [Management was] proposing an environment where people should offer their frank opinions and where executives could no longer hide in their big offices but had to engage in open debate with their teams.
e You have to be very committed to what you are going to do.
You have to be prepared to make some tough people decisions.

6 a competition b competitors c compete
d uncompetitive

7 a a innovative b innovation c innovation
d innovate e innovation/(innovative)
f innovator
b 1 b 2 e 3 a 4 c 5 f 6 d

B 3 a Project teams were set up with the aim of increasing communication across the different business units.
b The goal was to encourage and share new ideas, as well as increase cross selling.

4 b Kristina: Prevented from divulging information (which could be interpreted as lack of trust).
Juana: Can't always understand native speakers – they use complex expressions and speak quickly.
Tom: Response times to e-mails slow – but doesn't want to use phone.
c *Suggested answers*
- Arrange both virtual and face-to-face meetings and training sessions where different members can discuss how they are experiencing the change and work out ways to work together.
- Clarify what information can be shared and what cannot, and why this is.
- Stress the need for clarity when they talk to each other, draw up agreed guidelines (how often they will communicate, response times to e-mails, etc.).
- Define a group of people who would be responsible for supporting the communication process. This 'communication taskforce' has the goal of continually monitoring, getting feedback and improving things.
- Measure innovative ideas and results of collaboration, communicate how new ideas and solutions are being implemented.

5 a So are you saying
b Could we clarify
c Just to confirm, what you're saying
d When you say
e If I understand

6 a Firstly, I think we should agree on
b Can we establish the purpose
c We need to set down some rules
d We should explain the reason
e It must be clear who is responsible

C 2 a - Low margins
- Inefficient networks
- High costs
b He called a management meeting and told them they must act drastically and immediately. He divided the products and services into projects and put a team of key people in each project group who were responsible for solving the problems. He then made sure these people prioritised the actions to get fast results.
c He linked pay increases and bonuses to each individual's contribution to the financial success of the organisation.
d He made it clear what the dangers of not changing would be: *We forecast that if we didn't turn things around in three months, the company would be bankrupt. So I just called the management to a meeting and said, 'We have no time to reorganise. If costs are too high, we have to cut them; if routes are inefficient, we have to stop running them; and if revenue is too low, we have to increase our prices.' I just said this is what we must do and we must do it now, not tomorrow or the day after.*
e People became more results driven and took more responsibility.

3 1 f 2 c 3 a 4 d 5 e 6 b
4 a link b speak up c change d make e prioritise
5 a If we don't cut costs, profits will reduce.
   b If the company doesn't change urgently, it will fail.
   c If our country doesn't implement international trade agreements, it will lose business.
   d If our organisation doesn't look for new markets, sales will drop.

D 2 b formal dress c results-oriented
   d high-pressure atmosphere e high-quality brand
   f closed offices g strong values
   h hierarchical organisation i blame culture
3 a value b act/behave c changes
   d are not working e behaving/acting f enlist(ing)
   g celebrated h form/grow i grow/form
   j does not change

2 Why change?

A 2 a Growing Asian competition; couldn't beat competitors on price
   b They replaced stores with online purchasing.
   c Ineffective marketing
   d Sales increased by 40%.
   e Marketing, technology and developing new skills
   f Convincing the board to invest / take on exposure to debt
3 a a Our aim is b In order to achieve; We will do this c it's essential that we
4 a

threats	opportunities
growing Asian competition	online purchasing
low sales	new technology
ineffective marketing	computer-aided
exposure to debt	manufacturing (CAM)
high prices	developing new skills

5 a are facing; ignore b take; miss c identified
   d scans e find out f avoid g exploit

B 3 a It is weak financially and is contracting. This is because there aren't enough projects to guarantee future growth, there have been reductions in all their European markets, and governments and property investors have cut back.
   b A merger with a larger organisation (AKA)
   c Risks: Lose control over direction; get rid of remaining partners; employees will object
   Opportunities: growth; professional development; secure future; bigger global projects
4 1 b 2 a 3 c
5 a forecasting b environmental analysis
   c organisational strategy
6 a Let's consider b What if c we'd probably
   d Have you considered e are likely
   f I'm certain g it's essential

7

certainty	possibility
I'm sure	What if …?
I'm certain	we'd probably
it's essential	Have you considered that … might …?
	are likely

8 1 c 2 d 3 b 4 e 5 f 6 a
C 3 a In 1976
   b The popularity of digital cameras
   c *Suggested answer*: The development of a technology which has the potential to undermine your business by making your main products or services out of date
   d *Suggested answer*: Digital camera sales would have eaten into sales of camera film.
   e 1 No brand is 'future-proof'.
     2 Constant innovation is required in a turbulent world.
     3 Organisations need to become more agile, which requires flexibility and the ability to cope with constant change and fluctuation.
5 1 d 2 g 3 e 4 a 5 b 6 h 7 f 8 c
6 b Borders should have reduced the number and size of stores and (should have) invested more in an online strategy.
   c Habitat should have changed its business model or produced cheaper products.
   d Hollywood Video should have invested in a video-streaming channel.
   e Lehman Brothers shouldn't have borrowed so much and (shouldn't have) made loans to people who couldn't pay the money back.

D 2 1 d 2 a 3 c 4 e 5 b
3 a 1 b 3 c 2 d 4 e 5
5 *Suggested answers*
   a autocratic (In emergency situations, there is no time for discussion; action must be taken.)
   b participative (Innovation and creativity is fostered by freedom to discuss, debate and collaborate.)
   c paternalistic (This is the only employer; operative employees often have less control over their destiny; management has more responsibility to support the employees.)
   d tactical (You need to react to unpredictable situations and changing circumstances, so it's more difficult to be strategic in this context.)

Case study
2 *Suggested answers*
   a Fred should first arrange to speak to Mr Luó, who is the most senior person (the leader in the Chinese part of the organisation plays a key role: seniority is respected, and the most senior person should be addressed first) and he seems to have control (*we will have to adjourn the meeting*).
   b Fred could start by stressing that although some changes are needed, the need to preserve the high quality and reliability of the products and services that customers have come to expect is very important. This seems to be a point they can agree on based on the fact that change is accepted as a natural part of life, but it's necessary to move

carefully and to ensure that harmony and important elements of the old system are maintained. This is evidenced by Mr Zhèng's comment: *We believe it's very important to preserve our quality and reliability. The other points we will discuss.*

  c After putting his proposals to Mr Luó, Fred could let him discuss with his team (as decision-making is consensual, and the team needs time to discuss different proposals). Following that, he could ask Mr Luó for a meeting to plan the steps that need to be taken.

  d Fred should not be so participative (*Shen, you've recently graduated, haven't you? Didn't you study in the US? How would you feel about taking on some more responsibility? Can you tell us all what you think?*). He shouldn't have tried to single out Shen and certainly not offer him more responsibility when he is not his manager. He probably embarrassed Shen, especially as the senior managers were present. He shouldn't have expected a decision to be made there and then (*Are there any comments? Can we have a show of hands? Who's in favour?*). He may also need to accept that he has to be more tactical rather than strategic. (Time is cyclical and not linear, so the focus on setting objectives today for a future goal is seen differently. If the situation changes, the objectives and goals may need to change, therefore strategic planning is not favoured and flexibility needs to be built into planning.)

3 Communicating change

A **1** *Suggested answers*: explaining how the change will impact on people, asking for ideas, telling people what and when will change

  3 a top down
    b He says: 'In the end, the change was used as a way of getting rid of people, but they didn't want to tell us that. So now when I hear "change", I worry.'
    c To be more honest and open about the change process and its impact on people
    d collaboratively
    e He looks for threats and opportunities and brings this information to meetings with the team.
    f He has a good relationship with his boss and with the management, and the team is consulted when things are going to change, so he trusts his company.
    g delegated
    h Because change was managed by senior managers and external consultants.
    i It was refreshing because the CEO trusted Erika and her team to work out how they could change and to decide themselves how best to implement change. They were given responsibility and recognition – a more bottom-up approach.

  4 a tell b talk c involve d engage e invite
    f take part g Ask h come up with i agree
    j listen

  5 1 e 2 a 3 b 4 c 5 f 6 d

B **2** a Asking for opinions (pulling)
    b Yoko thinks they should tell staff as soon as possible that the company is in trouble.
    c He pushes to close and summarises the message to communicate to staff.
    d He wants to stress that although this means a big change in the way people work, jobs would be safe.

  3 a To motivate people, support them and set clear guidelines and goals
    b She thinks the proposals will take too much time and in the meantime, the company will run out of money.
    c She seems to favour a push approach (*We need to be clear and tell staff …*); there is no suggestion of asking for opinions. This is probably because the financial situation is serious and requires quick, decisive action.

  5

asking for opinions	I'd like to hear your views on what we can do to change. Where should we be going in the next three years? What can we do to change and survive?
showing you're listening	Thanks, Yoko. I agree that it's important to be open and honest with staff … So, you're saying that … people can be home-based …
committing to action	I'll produce a proposal for the May 15th meeting.
suggesting ideas	Can't we retrain people for different jobs? We could also use selected photos to produce professional videos with music …
recognising value	Our loyal workforce has been the key to our success up to now. Thanks for your contributions, you're a great team.
pushing communication to a close	Let's summarise and agree what we're going to communicate.

  6 a talk about things we are convinced about
    b agree to do or not do something
    c talk about possible futures
    d talk about consequences

C **3** a By e-mail
    b To tell them not to enter into financial transactions with third parties
    c Because of the loss of billions of dollars on risky mortgage-backed investments, and the failure to find a rescue plan for the firm.
    d They didn't expect it; they thought the firm would be rescued.
    e Only top management knew what was happening.
    f Not much – they complained about lack of information: *We're not trading and we're just kind of waiting to hear.*

g How quickly it happened; the pace of finance is very fast. Things can go very quickly, because institutions have such a high level of debt. If they can't pay interest or pay back loans on demand, they quickly go bankrupt.

5 a internal communication b handed out
c high-level information d update e uncertainty

6 a atmosphere b shock c We really didn't see this coming. d holding out hope e understanding
f disconsolate g acceptance

7 1 d 2 a 3 c 4 b

8 a The purpose of this b This is due to
c This means that d We are doing this to

D Case study

2 *Suggested answers*

a Guidelines
- Be clear about what outcome you want from the meeting (purpose).
- Facilitate communication by involving all participants, encouraging feedback and recognition of contributions (people).
- Make sure all contributions are summarised; delegate responsibilities and get agreement on actions (process).

b
- Culturally diverse / geographically dispersed
- Channels of communication – difficult to communicate face to face, so most communication will be telco, video conference or e-mail.
- The way you communicate (top down / collaboratively / delegating) needs to be carefully considered and discussed with a wide range of company representatives in order to choose the right approach for each context.
- Where possible, change should be delegated either to individuals or local management, as empowering people to implement change tends to be more effective.
- Communicating change may be delegated to local managers; it's important that these individuals are very clear about the overall message and important that all managers communicate consistently. It's very easy to send out mixed messages when there are multiple channels/communicators.
- Impact of change will be different depending on place and context. Important to create a channel where people can express opinions and give feedback on change and to adapt to local situation whilst staying focused on the goal.

4 Overcoming resistance

A 1 *Suggested answers*

a Fear of losing position/power/influence/ relationships/job; having new unfamiliar boss/ colleagues; insecurity about new systems/ processes/technology / need to use a foreign language; don't understand or agree with the reasons behind change; lack of clarity about the future; change of location/salary/conditions/ benefits, etc.

c Communicate frequently and clearly; stress benefits of change; ensure those implementing change are united and communicating same message; have regular meetings; represent and support people; listen to concerns; ask for regular feedback; coach and mentor; demonstrate strong leadership skills; model new behaviours and attitudes; influence others

2 a He feared losing power.
b Marco had the support of his department because he was loyal and represented them, so he could influence them regarding the change.
c The company offered to 'protect' his team in exchange for his support.

3 a He lost his 'sponsor' and therefore an important relationship.
b One-to-one discussions; established objectives to improve attitude and behaviour; he was fired.

4 a influencers b influence c influential
d influenced e influence f influence

5 a adapted b adapt c resisting d resist
e resistance

6 a into b behind c for d to e through f on

7 a with; about b about c to d through

B 3 a To help talk Rui through some problems (organisational changes and new process that have been introduced)
b Lack of clarity about Rui's role

4 a He's not sure how his role fits with what the others are doing, so he can't set goals. He also feels he needs more direction.
b Talk to Mr Schmidt, his team leader; ask for a team meeting to establish who is doing what; agree some targets.
c If the team has the meeting and manages to decide who is going to do what and by when, he'll see this as progress.
d FW Net set objectives and expect teams to be autonomous. Bamberg teams were given more direction.

5 a Can you prioritise
b What exactly
c Shall we
d What have you done so far
e How could you
f What could stop you
g What are you going to do
h how will you know

6 1 f 2 a 3 e 4 c 5 b 6 g 7 d

7 a loss of status or job security
b lack of reward system c fear of the unknown
d protecting interests of own group
e climate of mistrust f organisational politics
g fear of failure h bad timing

C 3 a '... to deal with the fall-out from the downsizing process, and move their organisations beyond the grief, the anger and the loss of morale that characterises these major organisational events. It is those that remain that will determine what happens to the organisation.'
b Do not pressurise employees to increase productivity or express feelings; talk about and listen to reactions in individual or group settings.

c Look after their own physical and emotional health; seek support if necessary.
  d 'Any shifting in staff will result in new challenges in terms of doing business, and there can be some confusion and chaos regarding how you are going to go about doing "business" with fewer people.'
  e Reduce the chaos; hold individual and group meetings; clarify what people should be doing.
4 b *Suggested answers*: frustrated, delighted, devastated, disappointed, optimistic
5 a pressurise b Ask c Show d Work e Take stock f hesitate; take g Address h Clarify i Problem-solve j Bring k Make sure l Create

D 5

task-oriented	relationship-oriented
recognising individual achievement	supporting work–life balance
setting financial goals	fostering teamwork
MBO (managing by objectives)	encouraging consensus decision-making
setting bonus-linked targets	giving reward for supporting others
focusing on returns for shareholders	arranging social or team-building events

Case study, Listening
  a The team doesn't seem to work, as they have many new members and they don't know each other.
  b The leader, Ben's, responsibility: *We suggested to you that we should all go out for a meal or something to get to know each other better, but you always seem too busy, so this still hasn't happened.*
  c He expects the team to be autonomous. They have the targets and they must find a way to achieve them.
  d She says they don't know what they should cut or how. They're a team and they all value different benefits, so they don't know who should have the authority to decide what they cut.
  e They're supposed to be working together and they don't like the idea of competing with each other, which he thinks is bad for morale.
  f Guillaume and Ellen prioritise relationships (*We suggested to you that we should all go out for a meal or something to get to know each other better / We're supposed to be working together here – what is this individual bonus about? Are we supposed to compete with each other? This is really bad for morale.*).
  Ben prioritises the task (*We have a big job to do. I expect my team to be autonomous. I've set the targets and it's up to you to find a way to achieve them.*).

Case study, Tasks
1 b, c, e
2 *Suggested answer*
  Guillaume's reaction to the individual bonus would indicate that it will not increase motivation ('Are we supposed to compete with each other? This is really bad for morale.'). However, Ben might want to find out more about the attitudes of other members of the team first, as Guillaume's response may not be representative of the whole team. It's important to establish what the key motivation of each team member is (financial, positive relationships, feeling part of a group, individual recognition/praise, etc.).
3 The three obstacles below may be easier to remove:
  • Unfamiliar leadership style (If the leader is perceived as more task focused, distant and less supportive, this could be changed by the leader adopting a more people/relationship-focused approach and increasing communication – showing interest in the family and welfare of people and having more regular contact: creating social media platforms; having more face-to-face meetings when possible.)
  • Not knowing the team members well (Set up calls / meetings / team-building events.)
  • Lack of clarity about roles/responsibilities/tasks (Clarify and agree through team meetings, etc.)
  The two obstacles below could be more difficult or take much longer to remove:
  • People not used to taking responsibility for targets (Creating a more autonomous culture will take more time and require leaders to gradually reduce direction as team members take more responsibility and become more proactive. It will also require consistent management behaviour in line with democratic leadership principles.)
  • Mismatch of values (e.g. target-oriented vs relationship-orientated cultures) (This could be removed by all involved taking part in intercultural training, observing differences in behaviour between different people and identifying the best points in different approaches to create synergy.)

5 Influencing people

A 2 a People who are naturally good salespeople, those who are well connected within networks in the company
  b Formal: cross-functional project groups
    Informal: triathlon team
3 a They make an effort to get to know new people; they listen and take an interest in them; they try to see the world through the eyes of others.
  b Communicate with a range of styles; identify people who need influencing, either because it's necessary to have them on board or because they're 'blockers'.
4 a keep in touch b put [people] in touch with c organise d bring [different groups] together e help f facilitate g build h networking i persuade
5 a connection b connecting/connected c connection d network e networking/networked f network g persuasion/persuader h persuasive i persuasive j facilitation/facilitator k facilitating l facilitation m include n inclusion o include p support q supportive r supportive s organisation/organiser t organised/organising/organisational u organiser
6 a network
  b facilitate/organise
  c facilitation/networking/organisational

Answer key

    d connection/organisation/facilitator/organiser/networker
    e persuasive/supportive/organised/inclusive
B 3 a Informally, in a friendly way – tries to make her feel comfortable by offering a coffee.
  b He gave her a useful contact, and this person helped her get her current position.
4 a To discuss the start date for implementing the new SCM software system
  b Her budget is stretched, and this new software implementation involves extra costs and staffing resources.
  c Yes, he is (*I'd like to hear your views and find out how you feel about this. / What extra costs exactly will you incur? / I hear what you're saying.*).
  d To reduce the order errors and returns by 20% in the next two years
  e He identifies how the software could help Consuela achieve her priority.
5 a Quick implementation of the system will help them both.
  b To divert the facilities budget to this project and to link staff bonuses to achievement of the implementation goals; also, Al will second one of his team to Consuela for six months.
  c Yes
6 a **a** disagreement **b** bargaining **c** consensus **d** disadvantage **e** proposal **f** leverage **g** benefits **h** compromise, concession **i** priorities
  b **a** concession/proposal **b** compromise/consensus **c** disadvantage **d** proposal **e** benefits/priorities/leverage **f** disagreement **g** bargaining
7 1 c, g, h
  2 a, e, f, m
  3 b, d, i, j, k, l
C 3 a It carried out a brand repositioning by upgrading the image, repositioning the flip-flops in stores, packaging them in boxes, introducing new colours and designs, and using sophisticated actors for advertising campaigns.
  b Simple pleasures, happiness and freedom
  c Products were placed near cleaning products, so maids could find them, and by building materials, for construction workers.
  d They were too embarrassed to wear them outside because they didn't portray the right image; the flip-flops were associated with poverty.
  e *Suggested answer*: They love them, they feel the product is part of their identity, their 'own brand', they connect with the 'image/story' around the brand.
  f *The brand has successfully associated itself with positive Latin American characteristics such as sensuality, youth and joy.*
    ... sold at Bloomingdale's and Neiman Marcus ... (= expensive, sophisticated stores)
    ... coveted by Hollywood actors such as Brad Pitt and Angelina Jolie, European royals and suburban ladies from Seattle to Seoul.
4 a brand **b** advertising **c** image
5 b advertising **c** upgraded/changed/improved **d** campaigns **e** transformation/repositioning **f** building/loyalty **g** image

D 2 a 3 b 1 c 2 d 3 e 1 f 2
3 a Create opportunities to meet people; use the phone rather than e-mail; choose behaviour that's comfortable for your international counterparts; listen and ask follow-up questions about the subjects that your partner talks about; find out what's important to them and take interest in these things.
  b Trust
  c Be more indirect in Latin American and Asian cultures than in Scandinavian ones.
  d The leader; someone who is influential because they have a strong network of contacts; someone with specialised knowledge; the majority

Case study, Listening
1 b 2 a, d 3 c

Case study, Tasks
1 To influence Marcio, Christina could: show some reverence and respect for him; try not to be too dominant; be strong without being aggressive; show that she recognises and values his knowledge and experience; learn from him; find out about the team from him, as he knows them better; give him a role in the implementation so that he's more in the forefront; stay in charge, but take more of a background role; support him and get his support so that he can be a sponsor for the project; show the other team members that she respects and trusts his authority.

To influence Claudia, Christina could: spend more time with her and the others socially; engage in weekend events and get to know her friends and family; listen to her more; ask her for advice; observe her style of communication; try to be more indirect; soften her approach – try to connect with the things she values; show that she trusts she can do the job; ask rather than telling.

To influence Rodrigo, Christina could: find out what work he is doing and why, and what his priorities are; find out what his main concerns are and try to address these; show interest in the local area and projects and find out if she can get involved in these; recognise the value of the work he is doing; try to address his stress and pressure by supporting him and coaching him regarding his workload; manage the projects, tasks; ask others to help and support.

6 Developing change leaders

A 3 a To be able to 'sell' the change across the organisation
  b She focused on learning to be more empathetic, trying to see things from other people's and other culture's perspectives.
  c She also learned to become more creative and innovative when looking for solutions.
4 a How to coach and mentor those who will have to leave and help them plan alternatives for the future
  b To define and delegate remaining roles and responsibilities clearly and motivate those people
  c Identifying what motivates people; giving and receiving feedback

d You have to be very resilient and you have to have confidence in yourself and in what you are doing.

8 b 4   c 7   d 1   e 5   f 3   g 9   h 8   i 6
9 a creative   b team-profiling   c compensate
d multiple ideas; comfort zone   e judgement
f feedback   g empower; innovate

B 3 a Karin says that she is pleased, as she met the targets (streamline processes, improve productivity, return unit to profit in six months).
b Bill has noticed that since the reorganisation, Karin has been working very hard to build a motivated team, with interesting new ideas coming from her people; they are starting to change the way they do things.
c She has lost a couple of good people.
d He wants her to listen more to people and to provide them with more support next time.
4 a There is a different working style to Germany.
b Bill thinks Karin would benefit from some coaching and mentoring development; some training on adapting her style; and more support and flexibility from him.
5 1 a, b, g
   2 c
   3 d, j
   4 e, f, i
   5 h
6 a review   b give   c tell   d do   e deal with   f think
g do   h try   i summarise
7 a 2   b 1   c 4   d 3
8 a *Suggested answers*
   a Juan, I don't think this report is up to the required standard. Can we go through it so we can identify some ways to improve it?
   b Mary, I'm concerned that your presentation, as it stands, isn't going to persuade the board. I suggest that you and I spend some together to think again about the objectives and how you can achieve them.
   c David, your e-mail came across as being very direct. Did you mean it to have that effect?
   d Yvonne, can I make some suggestions as to how you could improve the way you chair your meetings?
   The person giving the feedback might also want to ask questions to find out what the other person thinks about their performance and what ideas they have for improvement.

C 2 a T (*... coloured bar charts on the walls of American companies. [...] they are publicly charting individual targets and whether workers have reached their goals or not.*)
b F (*The general manager at the plant says that this is the most difficult thing for American workers to adapt to when they start working for Toyota North America. / When the general manager joined the company [...], she was shocked to find that the culture at Toyota was to expose problems in this way ...*)
c T (*It is during this preparation that some of the most prized corporate secrets are instilled in the future leaders. / ... where practices are so confidential that no outsiders are permitted entrance.*)
d F (*The executives are then sent off around the world to different offices as missionaries, charged with the task of spreading the 'Toyota way of working'.*)
e F (*... the* kaizen *mind (a constant sense of crisis which drives continuous improvement).*)
f F (*The founding of the 'Toyota Institute' is an attempt by the company to keep control and to manage growth, but it remains to be seen if this goal will be achieved.*)
5 a charting   **b** enlist   **c** founded   **d** prized   **e** diluted
f sprawling
6 a developing   **b** internationalisation
c keeping true   **d** infusing our philosophy
e teaching methods   **f** by word of mouth   **g** explicit
h to the same tune   **i** institution
j missionaries around the world   **k** our culture
l invest   **m** maintain

D 1 c *Suggested answer*: Culture can affect the style of feedback in a number of ways. Here are some examples:
• Some cultures may prefer a more critical and direct style of feedback; others may prefer a style which gives critical feedback more indirectly, and which focuses much more on giving positive feedback.
• In hierarchical cultures, feedback may go much more typically top-down, from boss to team member. In more egalitarian cultures, it may be possible for team members to comment directly on the performance of their manager.
• In more collectivist cultures, feedback may be given to the group rather than to the individual. In more individualist cultures, it may be common for feedback to be given to individuals in a very public way, e.g. employee-of-the-month awards.
2 a Because Petra criticised Ken, one of his sales team, in front of everyone at the meeting.
b It's a key factor in the improvement process: 'always prioritise the customer needs'.
c Petra is trying to improve the service so they can achieve their goal.
d She thinks that, for Petra, the feedback is constructive, not negative.
e For Ken, giving this kind of feedback in front of others means he loses face, which is especially critical in his culture.
f Jean-Claude will raise this issue at the next team meeting (to discuss expectations about feedback and how to give it).
3 *Suggested answers*
WHY: In our team, we believe that feedback is important because it's a great way for people to learn and to become higher performing.
WHO: In our team, feedback should be given by the team leader mostly, as they are responsible for managing performance.
WHEN/HOW: In our team, feedback should be given formally at team meetings – never by e-mail.
WHAT NOT: In our team, feedback is not an opportunity to attack another member of the team.

Case study

1 *Suggested answers*

a In order to assess the effectiveness of Mike's e-mail, first analyse the facts. He provides feedback quickly – the end of the same day on which the feedback was requested. The feedback is provided in a short and simple structure, and is positive in tone. This could lead to the interpretation that he took Paula's request seriously and so wanted to respond promptly. He may have wanted to communicate in a short and simple form in order not to impact on Paula's time too much. He knows she has many other things to do than just read his e-mails. And he delivers a message which seems to focus 100% on the positive – she is doing a good job, she just needs to continue doing that. However, he has clearly not addressed the frustrations Paula is experiencing with the other project members. Of course, Paula's reaction is not positive, so it can be argued that the e-mail is not effective, as it creates anger and confusion. But how far that is the fault of the e-mail or the responsibility of Paula is open to question.

b Paula's reaction is typical of many professionals when reading e-mails which do not meet their expectations. She reads it mainly from her own perspective and values – it's not what she wanted or would have written and, therefore, it is bad. Paula may need to develop a more open-minded approach to others' communication, and try to reflect on their intentions rather than expecting them to conform to her expectations. She should also take feedback from the e-mail that she did not clearly communicate to Mike in her request what exactly she wanted. If she had been more explicit, Mike may have communicated to her in a style and with content which she wanted.

There may also be an underlying difference in approach to feedback here, arising from culture or personality or both. Mike could be using a more indirect and positive/praising style of feedback as a general rule. It's possible that Paula expects a more direct and critical form of feedback – she is open to that and so tends to see praise as superficial and meaningless.

Paula could have been more proactive about the other issues she is concerned about. She could have arranged a meeting herself with the other team members to raise the issue directly, after informing Mike. Perhaps he wants the team members to be more autonomous and to try to solve their own problems before he gets involved. However, he could have made this clear to her in the e-mail if this was the case. Perhaps his communication is too indirect for Paula.

c Firstly, Mike should have clarified the intentions behind Paula's original request with a few questions, for example, 'What kind of feedback are you looking for?' and 'Shall we do this by e-mail, or is it better to do this face to face?'. Once he had clarified the style and content of feedback expected, he would have been in a better position to communicate. If he decided that he still wanted to use e-mail rather than a telephone call, it would have been good for him to signal at the end of his message a clear openness and availability to discuss further: 'If you would like to discuss this feedback in more detail, or to raise other questions with me, I am more than happy to schedule a telephone call with you.'

He should also have indicated what actions he would take in respect of Paula's concerns about the team and progress of the project, to make it clear that he was listening to her; for example, he could have said he would arrange a meeting with the team members. Alternatively, he could have suggested that she arrange a meeting to address the concerns directly with the team as a first step, also explaining that he would like the team to develop strategies to manage problems themselves.

2 a
- Lack of communication and feedback on communication between Paula and Silvio is starting to cause conflict. Communication and feedback protocols haven't been agreed in advance.
- Beatriz needs support, but is too afraid to ask for it. Perhaps in her context, asking for help is perceived as a sign of weakness. Unfortunately, this means that she hasn't completed her task, and this is perceived by others as a failure to do what she said she would. Levels of support needed to enable team members to complete the different tasks have not been accurately assessed.
- Rudolf is waiting for Mike to complete an action, as he feels it is not his responsibility to sign off this part of the project. Responsibilities haven't been clearly defined.

b Mike could help them develop the following skills: communication skills, team understanding, roles and responsibilities, support and feedback. Also, intercultural skills to help them understand difference in styles and to see each other's point of view, to listen before judging.
He could also improve his own skills in giving direction and empowering others.

c He could facilitate a meeting and ask each team member to explain how they feel the project is going and explain any issues they are having. He could then make sure agreement is reached around these areas:
- Communication: They could establish protocols about how they should communicate (by e-mail, phone, etc.), how often and agree response times.
- Team understanding: The team members should listen to and understand each others' position and together find ways forward, addressing each issue in turn. They should find out what is important to each person and build relationships.
- Roles and responsibilities: Clearly define what role and responsibilities each member has, what is expected and by when; who has

authority to make what decisions; and check that each member is happy that they are capable of carrying out the tasks or if they need some support.
- Support: Check that all team members understand that they can and should ask for support if they feel they will not be able to complete a task in time or to the right standard. Also encourage team members to ask for support if they feel stressed or pressured. Encourage all team members to support each other when possible.
- Feedback: Feedback is particularly critical in international teams as a way of clarifying misunderstandings among people with different values and forms of behaviour. They could collectively complete and commit to a set of statements about the feedback culture which they would like.

E *Sample answer*
Dear Mike
Many thanks for your e-mail. I think there may be a little misunderstanding and perhaps I did not communicate clearly what I was looking for in terms of feedback.
My first objective is to learn about ways I can improve, so I would be very happy to hear any critical comments which you think would help me to learn and develop.
I would also like you to consider more seriously my feedback to you on the progress of the project. I would like to discuss what actions can be taken in order to move the project forward, as I am concerned that we are behind schedule.
Could we schedule a phone call to discuss, as this will also enable me to ask you questions on specific areas about which I would like feedback? I can also explain in more detail my concerns about the project.
I am available before 11:30 CET every day next week.
Look forward to hearing from you.

7 Evaluating and measuring

A 3 a He used SMART objectives.
  b People feel judged if measurement is done by a small group. Everyone should take credit for success and responsibility for fixing mistakes.
  c Legal requirements
  d Targets related to following technical procedures
4 a Behaviour you can see, feedback you can hear, experiences you can feel, numbers you can count
  b Levels of ethical behaviour
  c You have to understand the complexities of the situation.
  Listen to local managers
  Don't be too quick to judge (based on your own experience).
  Build more flexibility into your targets.
6 1 e 2 a 3 b 4 d 5 c
7 a define **b** set **c** feel **d** get **e** hide **f** blame
  g decide on **h** take **i** measure **j** ensure
8 a adherence **b** compliance **c** protection
  d following **e** interviews; commitment **f** levels
  g filling **h** reduction **i** innovative
  j quantitative; motivation; qualitative

B 2 **S**pecific, **M**easurable, **A**chievable, **R**elevant, **T**ime-bound
3 a The goal is clear and unambiguous. Goals must tell a team exactly what's expected, why it's important, who's involved and where it's going to happen.
  b It helps a team stay on track, reach its target dates and experience the sense of achievement that motivates it to to reach the ultimate goal.
  c The attitudes, skills and financial capacity to reach it
  d Because you need support to accomplish a goal: resources, a champion, someone to remove obstacles.
  e Because they help a team focus their efforts on completion of the goals and prevent goals from being overtaken by the day-to-day crises that invariably arise in an organisation.
5 a achievable **b** relevant **c** specific **d** time-bound
  e measurable
6 a How will you know if you are successful?
  b What does success mean in relation to this goal?
  c What does success mean to different people?
  d What can you measure?
  e Are the goals realistic?
  f Have you considered all the possible obstacles?
  g Are the goals relevant to your organisation?
  h Will you receive that needed support?
  i What milestones and deadlines will you set?
7 a retrospect **b** think **c** reflection **d** Would
  e exactly **f** hindsight

C 3 A 4 B 1 C 2 D 3
4 a They enable executives to hear from staff directly, without having messages filtered through intermediate management levels; they have flattened the organisational hierarchy; they have driven positive culture shifts.
  b By monitoring and participating in online discussions, managers can more readily see where any misunderstandings or 'pain points' exist across the enterprise and take steps to address them.
  c Networks like Twitter, Yammer and Facebook can help employees: get information about new processes or technologies; share innovative practices; and receive answers in timely ways.
  d They can help by providing near real-time feedback about how well a programme is going.
5 a collaborative culture **b** hierarchy
  c culture shifts **d** communications medium
  e 'pain points' **f** mechanism **g** real-time feedback
  h timely information **i** knowledge networks
  j innovative practices

D 1 He wants more IT centralisation and a greater focus on innovation.
2 *Suggested answers*
  Centralisation can be measured in numbers, e.g. setting targets to see a reduced number of different IT systems and software used in the organisation.

Innovation can also be measured in numbers, e.g. setting up and running a specific number of cross-border innovation projects with a calculated financial benefit to the organisation. You can also measure the impact innovations have on sales or customer perception, e.g. through asking how people feel in customer surveys.

3 a Centralisation targets are easier to quantify; they have quantitative results and are centrally driven/funded. Innovation programmes faced resistance, as co-operation is more difficult to achieve, especially getting mature markets to collaborate, as they are risk averse and more structured (not so flexible).
   b Through customer surveys – asking questions about customer satisfaction and how customers feel – more qualitative data
   c Drawing on global expertise to gain competitive advantage

Case study

1 a People working in local organisations often respond quite negatively when they receive communication from headquarters about proposals to change their way of working, especially when new procedures seem to involve more reporting (more work) to headquarters. It is often felt to be a loss of autonomy and a lack of trust in local expertise.
      However, Ron may respond positively. Better project management tools can potentially help him to do his job in Canada much more effectively.
   b There is no single right way to respond. It's important for Ron not to respond too negatively too quickly, until he understands the implications of the changes and how far the central organisation will provide funding to help local organisations to change. The best response is probably to welcome the intention behind the initiative, but to seek more clarity on the details and the budget implications.
2 a The lack of trust
   b To use sophisticated project management tools – people are not sufficiently trained.
   c She disagrees. She thinks a new approach is necessary to improve currently poor levels of project management in the company.
   d Becauses he thinks he is losing flexibility – giving up control of key projects. He also thinks it will generate a lot of work and that the metrics are too mechanical and will stop people thinking about quality.
3 Some of Ron's arguments may be true. Sometimes headquarter-driven change initiatives can cause a lot of work and focus on metrics which don't really help local operations to deliver more quality. If this is the case here, it may be that Ron is right to try to kill the idea very early with strong, negative feedback. But we don't know enough about Ron's organisation to pass a real judgement on Ron's response. The planned changes may be badly needed. 'Fighting' may be the wrong strategy and make senior management see him as obstructive and not supporting internationalisation, which could damage his career prospects.
4 For this task, decide on a message (positive, negative or balanced) which you think Ron should communicate to Fabio and then plan your arguments accordingly. There is no single right way to do this. It's an opportunity to practise responding in a presentation to change initiatives from headquarters.

8 Cultural shifts

A 3 a over 12 years
    b He found it almost impossible to change the attitudes and practices of the (ageing, conservative, white male) management team.
    c She is a woman and she is from Japan.
    d To devise a global HR strategy to develop more diverse and creative teams
  4 a Compatible policies for reward and promotion
    b About five years ago, when the people who were blocking change were finally replaced
    c Be resilient, patient and persistent – convey the message that change will happen.
    d You have to go through the steps (you need a lot of time); people need to see positive results.
  5 a allow b go through c demonstrate d change
    e look for f rethink
  6 a diverse workforce b different perspectives
    c family-friendly policies d jobs and family
    e employee rotation f take risks g autonomy
    h company-wide training programmes
    i compatible with diversity goals
  7 b More analytical thinker: logical, objective, planned, specific, realistic, focus on quantitative data, intellectual, structured
       More creative thinker: intuitive, impulsive, holistic, free, imaginative, emotional, focus on qualitative data, subjective

B 3 1 c 2 b 3 a
  4 1 ethos 2 logos 3 pathos
  6

addition	contrast
as well as, furthermore, in addition, like, similarly	although, contrary to, despite, however, nevertheless, on the other hand, unless, unlike, whereas

  7 a However / Nevertheless / On the other hand
    b unless
    c Furthermore / In addition
    d Despite
    e Unlike
  8 *Suggested answers*
    1 a, i, o, p
    2 b, d, h, j
    3 c, e, k, q
    4 c, f, g, l, m, n, r

C 3 a Companies with a blend of male and female senior executives are more successful, both economically and in terms of their corporate culture.

    b Of the 13 members of the board, five are female and all five are mothers of young children.
    c A family-friendly environment
    d Because it organises and helps pay for daycare centres, operates a parents' and babysitters' exchange and pays agency fees for all kinds of family services. Job solutions are customised for women returning to work after maternity leave. The company provides technical equipment for those employees who wish to work at home, and employees on maternity or paternity leave are copied in on important documents to keep them in the loop.
    e The notion that it should be possible to send an employee anywhere at any time, and the corporate requirement for undivided attention
    f The company gives preferential treatment in the hiring process to women with the same qualifications as men applying for the same positions.
    g Acceptance among senior executives; management must actively support and aggressively promote the goal of promoting women managers.

4 a a blend of male and female senior executives
    b a family-friendly environment
    c to keep [them] in the loop
    d incompatible with
    e preferential treatment
    f performance review

5 a performance b supervisor(s) c preferential treatment d recruiting e treat f promoting g Customise h equipment i employees

D 4 1 b 2 c 3 d 4 a

    5 *Suggested answers*
    As this is a big change for Martha, she could:
- take part in some intercultural training to raise her own awareness
- use the suggested guidelines to help her guide the team
- bring the team together for a training session/event where they all examine their own cultures, similarities and differences. Expectations of teamwork could be discussed, and together they could agree a way to work together. This is sometimes called creating 'a cultural island' where a new 'team culture' is created.

Once Martha has achieved team understanding, to make sure the team is effective in the longer term, she could make the most of the diversity of the team to react to changes in the global environment and to identify different ideas. She could motivate and encourage the team to innovate by giving them autonomy; in the end, she must demonstrate positive results.

Case study

2 Maria has strengths in relation to points 1, 4 and 5.
Stanley has strengths in relation to points 2, 4, 5 and 6.
Samantha has strengths in relation to points 1, 2 and 3.

3 The question is do you take Samantha, because she has more higher-priority strengths, or Stanley as he has a broad range of strengths? Stanley would be the safer bet, but Samantha fits the profile of the change the company wants to see – more diversity, more women, more entrepreneurial. Therefore, the best choice would be Samantha.

Answer key

Word list

acceptance	32
adapt (successfully) to	18
adapt a message	58
adapt to change	9
(piece of) advice	8
appoint (someone to a job position)	82
authoritative	80
barrier	18
bonus-linked targets	44
brainstorm (ideas)	24
brainstorming (meeting/session)	84
build rapport	48
centralised decision-making	14
chaos	8
clarify	40
coaching	40
collaborative(ly)	28
collective responsibility	63
come up with (an idea / a solution)	29
(inside/outside your) comfort zone	59
commit to (something)	64
common ground	50
common/shared goals	59
communication channels	10
company-wide	79
compensate for weaknesses	59
competence	29
competitive edge	9
complacent	13
compliance	69
compromise	51
computer aided manufacturing (CAM)	19
concession(s)	51
consensus	50
consequences	19
consolidate change	78
convince (someone)	50
cope (to be able to)	47
culturally diverse	35
define a target	68
delegated	28
deliver results	12
develop (a product/skills)	24
disruptive innovation	23
diverse workforce	79
downsize/downsizing	42
draw up (a schedule / an agenda)	50
emerging (markets/economies)	9
emotional connection	53
empower (someone)	59
enable (someone to do something)	59
encourage (networking/innovation)	48
ethical challenge	68
evidence(-based)	80
expansion (strategy)	10
explore (possibilities/options/ alternatives)	41
external threat	18
face an issue	18
face-to-face	65
facilitate (a meeting / a call)	49
fall short of (target)	69
(a piece of) feedback	10
financial reward	44
flatten (a hierarchy)	72
flow of ideas	9
focus on (goals/targets)	60
formal/informal network	48
fresh perspective	85
frustration	39
gain (experience / market share)	25
geographically dispersed	35
get clarification	35
get to know (someone)	53
give feedback	58
give/make a speech	80
go through a process	79
goal-setting (set goals)	70
grievance	29
(draw up) guidelines	11
harmonious	29
(with) hindsight	70
identify (an opportunity)	19
ignore (a threat)	19
(the) impact (of something on)	8
implement change	8/10
in trouble	30
incompatible with	82
increase (your) visibility	48
influencer	48
infuse a philosophy	62
innovate	22
innovation-driven	9

inspire	80
integrate	68
interim manager	12
involve people	68
keep someone informed	33
lack of (information/resources)	32
large-scale change	73
leadership (style)	45
legacy	81
make an effort	55
make sense	75
make someone accountable for	13
make someone aware of (something)	48
march to the same tune	62
match (someone's style)	34
maternity leave	83
measure change	68
measure success	40
mentoring	59
merge (with)	38
metrics	75
mismatch (of values)	45
monitor (a process)	11
motivate (staff/employees)	13
objection (to change)	21
obstacles	70
on the same wavelength	51
online retailing	23
outcome	30
outline (benefits/content)	51
overcome (resistance/problems/ barriers)	40
participative (management) style	24
persuasion strategy	53
praise (someone)	67
predict	24
present (a vision)	25
present the case for	28
preserve benefits	29
prioritise	68
protect (interests)	32
provide feedback	35
pull (communication)	30
push (communication)	30
put someone in touch with (someone)	49
qualitative	69
quality standards	63
quantitative	69
rate of change	18
react	42
reassure	41
recognise value	41
recommendations	75
reduce staff numbers	43
redundancies	38
reposition	53
represent (team/department)	58
resist change	38
resolve conflict	58
rethink attitudes	78
risk-averse	74
run out of (money/time)	31
scenario-planning	20
sense of urgency	12
short-term gain	81
show empathy	41
SMART (goals/tools)	68
speak up (about something)	13
spread change	48
staff morale (high/low)	44
staff survey	63
stakeholder(s)	69
strategic thinking	25
streamline	15
summarise (key points)	56
sustainable	69
take advantage of	58
take risks	74
think outside the box	85
timeframe	69
to treat women equally	83
top-down	22
track change	73
transform	53
turnaround	12
upgrade (a system / software)	53
virtual team	60
vision	18
voluntary redundancy	42
waste (time/money/resources)	75
word of mouth	62
work through (process)	39
workers' rights	69

Word list

International Management English

International Management English consists of four titles covering key aspects of international business operations: *Leading People*, *Managing Projects*, *Managing Change* and *Working Virtually*. These four titles provide insights into the challenges of working internationally and develop practical skills which will help people to do their jobs more effectively.

Each book in the series consists of eight units, with every unit offering four distinct sections:

- *Discussion and listening* Engaging and relevant content in areas of international management and teamwork.
- *Communication skills* In addition to the familiar topics of meetings, presentations and negotiations, input and practice are also provided in conflict management, team building and giving and receiving feedback.
- *Professional skills* Authentic texts from management writers and thinkers provide the starting point for reflection and discussion among learners.
- *Intercultural competence* A focus on raising cultural awareness followed by an illustrative case study.

Leading People
by Steve Flinders

This helps new and experienced managers to develop leadership skills for working and communicating internationally.

ISBN 978-1-905085-67-5

Managing Projects
by Bob Dignen

This provides practical ideas on how to work and communicate effectively when taking part in or leading international projects.

ISBN 978-1-905085-66-8

Managing Change
by Fiona Mee

This focuses on the communication requirements of those either taking part in or leading business change, including how to handle resistance.

ISBN 978-1-905085-68-2

Working Virtually
by Jackie Black and Jon Dyson

This addresses the communication challenges that global teams face when using information technology to collaborate.

ISBN 978-1-905085-69-9

For full details of this series, please visit the Delta Publishing website:
www.deltapublishing.co.uk